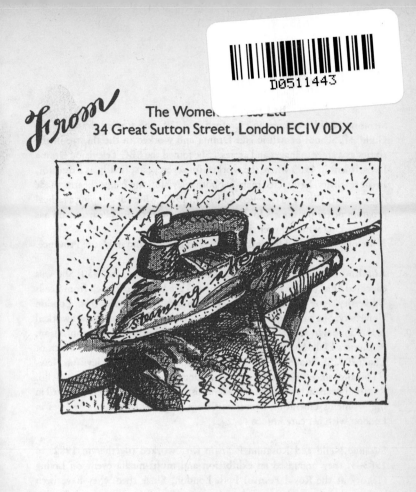

Women Like Us

Suzanne Neild was born in Hereford in 1939. She studied drama at the Guildhall School of Music and Drama and worked in the theatre in the sixties as a stage manager and actress. She joined the BBC Television Drama Department in 1963 where she worked for seven years, finally as a director. In the seventies she directed plays for both television and fringe theatre, made documentary films and travelled widely. In 1982, whilst developing a radical programme for pensioners for Channel 4, she met Rosalind Pearson and has been working with her ever since.

A lifelong lesbian and feminist, she lives in London and in Haute Provence.

Rosalind Pearson was born in Blackburn, Lancashire, in 1950. She was educated at a convent grammar school and graduated in French from Leeds University, later taking an MA in social and cultural studies from London University. She has taught in the UK and abroad and for several years worked as the campaign and research worker for a radical pensioners' organisation, Pensioners Link. She started work in television in 1982 with the launch of Channel 4. She works on a freelance basis for Independent Television News (ITN) and, since 1984, has been making documentaries with Suzanne Neild. Rosalind Pearson is a lesbian and a feminist and has been actively involved in the Women's Liberation Movement since the early seventies. She lives in London with her cat, Amber.

Suzanne Neild and Rosalind Pearson first worked together in 1982. In 1983–4, they organised an exhibition and multi-media event on Living History at the Royal Festival Hall London. Since then, they have been making documentaries on older women's lives as partners in their own independent production company, Clio Co-op.

Clio Co-op. is committed to furthering the study of oral history, demanding more positive images of ageing, promoting feminist issues and combating ageism.

WOMEN LIKE US

Suzanne Neild
&
Rosalind Pearson

The Women's Press

First published in Great Britain by The Women's Press Ltd, 1992
A member of the Namara Group
34 Great Sutton Street,
London EC1V 0DX.

© Suzanne Neild and Rosalind Pearson, 1992

The right of Suzanne Neild and Rosalind Pearson to be identified as the
authors of this work has been asserted by them in accordance with the
Copyright, Designs and Patents Act, 1988.

British Library Cataloguing in Publication Data
A catalogue record for this book is available from the British Library

ISBN 0 7043 4285 5

Typeset by Contour Typesetters, Southall, London
Printed and bound in Great Britain by
BPCC Hazell Books
Aylesbury, Bucks, England
Member of BPCC Ltd.

ACKNOWLEDGMENTS

We would like to thank all the older lesbians who generously gave us their time, their trust and their stories and without whom this book would not exist.

Our thanks, also, to Lis Whitelaw for her enthusiasm, support and constructive comments during the editing process; to Katherine Bright-Holmes, our editor at The Women's Press, for her help in the later stages of editing; and to Caroline Spry, our commissioning editor at Channel 4 Television, for her determined commitment to lesbian broadcasting.

And a final thanks in gratitude to all at the Lesbian Archives whose original copies of Arena 3 and Sappho provided many happy hours of reading and who helped us in our pursuit of older lesbians willing to share their stories with us.

CONTENTS

During the making of the television documentary *Women Like Us* we were asked many times to explain what we were doing and why. Sometimes it was very difficult to keep on saying the words 'older lesbians', not knowing what the response might be. It varied a lot. There was latent and overt homophobia on one side, sometimes including an ageist and patronising element, and on the other side, an inspirational enthusiasm. What became clear was the ignorance and lack of information about the lives and existence of older lesbians, and the strong wish to know more. It was for these reasons that we were making the documentary.

Television is a very accessible means of reaching a wide audience and can make people think and question assumptions in a direct and immediate way. As Ruth, one of the interviewees, says at the beginning of the programme, 'Let's face it, if you met me in the street, you wouldn't say "Hah, that is a lesbian" would you?' This simple statement, together with the image of a curly-haired older woman walking along a cliff path, immediately confounds some people's stereotypical image of a lesbian. To see sixteen very different older lesbians on television confronts a lot of unquestioned assumptions and raises many interesting issues. The disadvantage is that a fifty-minute film cannot deal with every issue in depth. Some things are bound to be left out or condensed. Also, unless the programme is repeated, or you have a copy of the video, you cannot refer to it again. This book is a way of filling in the gaps, extending the stories and providing more information. We hope it will also generate more interest in older women's history in general and lesbian history in particular.

INTRODUCTION

That ageism is a strong force in modern society comes as no surprise to most of us. Young is the thing to be – it's where the ideas are, where the power lies and certainly where the style is. Consequently, the media is not interested in older women – they are not considered newsworthy, not 'attractive' and have only a past to offer! To many, even that important past can be negated and diminished. For example, our documentary on women's work for peace since 1915, where twenty old women relate their peace activities this century, was reviewed in *Time Out* (8 June 1988) as 'a succession of game old birds reminisce about their salad days when they non-aggressively fought for peace'. Such distortion of old women's lives is commonplace. On the rare occasions that their existence is acknowledged, the image is generally stereotyped. And, as this review shows, if the image does not fit the stereotype, some people can't see the reality through their own ageist assumptions.

But if old women are rarely visible in the media, old lesbians have totally ceased to exist. There may be many reasons for this, but sex is certainly an important part of this cloak of invisibility. The image of lesbians shaped for us by the media is generally a sexual one, otherwise there is no reason for us to be acknowledged. Obviously, in the media's eyes, old women have no sexuality, every old woman automatically becomes a 'granny', (and, therefore, heterosexual), irrespective of the reality. Therefore, it follows there are no lesbians! Not only the media is guilty of these ageist assumptions. It merely reflects what many of us think (or more revealingly, don't think) about old women in general. The stereotypes are narrow and extremely diminishing. Most people do not expect old people to hold radical views and when they do, they are regarded as endearing eccentrics. Similarly, they are not expected to have a future, or to seek change, and the notion of their sexual desire produces embarrassed laughter.

Lesbians are as guilty as the rest when it comes to the worship of youth. Even being thirty is considered a major obstacle, and we often don't think to include images of old lesbians in the things we produce. Yet age is a natural progression of all our lives; and we have to confront the contradictions and the prejudices we all feel towards the old women we are becoming. If we do not, then we become a party to the devaluation of our very selves. As Baba Copper eloquently says in *Ageism in the Lesbian Community* (The Crossing Press, 1987):

> 'Unless old lesbians are re-membered as sexual, attractive, useful, integral parts of the woman-loving world, then current lesbian identity is a temporary mirage, not a new social statement of female empowerment.'

If we do not look at history and the present through the eyes of older women, not only do we get a distorted view of the past, but it reinforces the notion that nobody has ever felt or experienced the things we are going through now; that somehow our concerns have sprung from nowhere; that no one struggled before us to make our lives easier; that old women do not exist.

With these thoughts in mind, we set ourselves up as Clio Co-op in 1984. Since then, we have been making documentary videos *with* older women, about their lives and experiences. We believe it is

12

essential to validate the contribution that ordinary older women have made, and are still making, to our history and to our present. Our lives have been enriched and inspired in so many ways through all the women we have met and who have shared their lives with us.

The same applies, perhaps even more urgently, to us as lesbians. If we do not safeguard and value our history, then we risk generation after generation believing that they are the first to do this, to feel that or to struggle against our oppression. It is vitally important that we record our lesbian history, so that our existence and our concerns are not obliterated. If not, we will be forgotten, rewritten and often misrepresented. Let us hope that future generations will not have to speculate on lesbian lives and that they will have the chance to learn from our diverse experiences.

For a long while, we had wanted to make a documentary with older lesbians – to show the reality and the diversity of our lives and our lesbian history. This desire was made all the stronger because there were no documentaries in this country about older lesbians. We also thought it was important to deal only with the lives of lesbians. Too often our history is linked with that of gay men. We believe there are distinct differences in that history – for instance, differences in experience, oppression and the fact of being women in a patriarchal world – this linkage has tended to obscure lesbian experience.

From our initial research, it became clear that society's attitudes to lesbianism has had a direct effect and influence on how lesbians see and saw themselves. Thus, in the suffragette period and immediately after the First World War, women's close friendships were acknowledged, but lesbianism was never mentioned. From then on, there has been a series of peaks and troughs in attitudes to homosexuality. With the popularisation of the sexologists' writings, there was a swing towards an extremely negative image of lesbianism, and this resulted in an abundance of literature and psychological studies highlighting the unseemly, immoral and unwholesome lesbian condition.

The banning of Radclyffe Hall's *The Well Of Loneliness* in 1928 provided a daily platform in national newspapers for rabid homophobia. The *Sunday Express* at the time described 'the book that must be suppressed' as 'a seductive and insidious piece . . . designed to display perverted decadence as a martyrdom inflicted upon these outcasts by a cruel society . . . It flings a veil of sentiment over their depravity'. The editor also insisted that he would rather 'give a healthy boy or a healthy girl a phial of prussic acid than this novel'. A stereotype of a lesbian had emerged in full force.

Our interviews with women who remember this time show that it has been a formative influence throughout their lives. For example, Rachel (born 1909) says in her story, 'Lesbian is a dirty word. It's bracketed with slime, muck, the devil – all the other dirty words you can think of. It's been a bad word right up to recently. I even find it difficult to use now'.

With the onset of the Second World War, women's close friendships once again became much more acceptable and the public fear of lesbianism declined.

The post-Second World War period and the fifties, in particular, brought probably one of the hardest times for lesbians. It became a 'no-win' situation. Psychological studies tried to find causes and cures. They wrestled with the 'nature and nurture' arguments and, generally, concluded that lesbians were 'made' – they had too close/too distant relationships with their parents; their mother was dominant/their father was dominant; they were immature and not fully developed, and so on. But the only real conclusion was that the lesbian condition was a deeply unhappy state.

There was, of course, an identifiable lesbian sub-culture which frequented such clubs as the legendary Gateways in Bramerton Street, London SW3.[1] For some lesbians, these clubs were a refuge from the homophobic world outside, a meeting with their own kind. At the same time, this lesbian sub-culture had its own rigid codes of behaviour where the roles of butch and femme became the key to belonging. As Pat James says in her story 'That was the way it was, and if you weren't one way or the other, if you didn't conform, they derided you for it.' Or as another interviewee, who first went there in 1957 says, 'There was no sort of cross-dressing. A butch would never dream of putting make-up on. A feminine girl wouldn't ask a butch girl to dance, it always had to be the other way round. I found these unspoken rules a little bit heavy sometimes.' When she questioned these roles, she felt she was 'letting the side down'.

But it would be wrong and unfair to say that all lesbians participated in this particular sub-culture. Some lesbians were completely unaware of it, others chose not to join in, yet others felt completely alienated by it. Jackie Forster says 'Lesbian in the fifties, as I understood it, was just a short back and sides woman with a waistcoat and all and I never saw myself like that. And so I didn't identify as lesbian at all.'

The sixties brought the beginnings of a liberalisation of attitudes towards lesbians. There were attempts to understand the 'twilight world of this lesbian existence'. A *Man Alive* documentary and other television programmes like *Women Without Men* were made and popular magazines, such as *Tit Bits*, devoted several pages to lesbian life. These attempts, on the whole, were naïve and the harsh stereotype was hardly dimmed (for example, the film *The Killing of Sister George* portrays its main character as a domineering, tweed-suited, butch lesbian) but there was a sympathy for the lesbian condition, albeit somewhat patronising. At the same time, dress codes became much less rigid, as unisex clothing became fashionable.

The Gay Liberation Front and the Women's Liberation Movement brought a higher profile and made lesbianism more open and acceptable. Information and help proliferated – at least in the big cities – in the form of magazines, leaflets, meetings and, later, lesbian and gay phone lines. As Sally says in her story, 'I accepted my lesbian position at a time when it was easier to do so, and so I thought "Well, blow that for a laugh, I don't want all this kind of closet business. You might as well say what you are".'

As we enter the last decade of the century – attitudes are changing once again. There is an acknowledgment of the existence of and discrimination against lesbians and gay men but at the same time an increase in repressive legislation against us. For some, however, the predatory, butch lesbian has never changed. It is a myth and a stereotype that is all too easily invoked.

We believe it is important to understand our continuing lesbian existence and to store it in words, pictures and film. If we do not, our history will be rewritten by a future generation who never knew us and we risk becoming invisible once again.

After we had done considerable research, Channel 4 agreed to fund our documentary in 1988. Things came together all at once. The Tory Government's Clause 28[2], seeking to ban 'the promotion of homosexuality', reared its head and Channel 4 responded with a commitment to promote lesbian and gay programming. This was one of the few positive things to come out of such repressive legislation.

We wanted to make a documentary which reflected the lives of all older lesbians in this country – from different races, regions, class backgrounds, with and without disabilities, and living in a variety of situations. It is important to see older lesbians leading lives full of joy, pain, anger, sadness, happiness, discussing politics, social life, lovers, current affairs and the future, enjoying the present and relating their past.

As film-makers, we realise that it is not that simple to make a documentary which accurately reflects these lives. There are many obstacles lying in wait, not least of which is the difficulty of 'coming out' on television, whatever your age. There are all sorts of decisions to make before agreeing to appear on television.

We have to remember that many lesbians have been forced to lead an existence unacknowledged by friends, families, neighbours and work colleagues; that some fear the effects on their families and friends if they are open about their sexuality on television. Some Black women may not want to take on board anti-lesbianism as well as the racism they have to deal with on a daily basis; some 'out' older lesbians have gone back into the closet because limited mobility has made them more vulnerable to the homophobia of their neighbours. And so it goes on. It is crucial to represent these lives in some form, to show the pressures placed on all of us by the heterosexist society in which we live. The voices of these women, if not their faces, speak out for all who have been silenced.

The way we work as film-makers is to spend a lot of time getting to know the women whom we will go on to film. It works better, there is an interaction taking place, and it feels much more reciprocal. In this way, we hope to develop a lot of trust. This trust is essential because we are dealing with women's personal experiences which form the foundation of their identities.

Although the trust may exist with us, it may be a different matter when the programme is broadcast, and their faces appear in households all around the country. This is true for anybody who appears on television. You have no control over how people will receive you, whether they will understand you, like you, agree with you or, indeed, recognise you. This is particularly difficult for those who choose to be heard and not seen in a programme, and can result in considerable anxiety. We can only be continually thankful and forever indebted to those who will take that step and appear, unsolicited sometimes, in many people's homes via the television set.

The Lesbian Archives and Information Centre has been an invaluable resource for us in our work on this project. We have spent many happy hours reading through the first homosexual magazines, such as *Urania*, produced by Esther Roper and Eva Gore-Booth in the 1910s and 20s and the first lesbian magazine *Arena 3*, which was started in 1963 by Diana Chapman, Esmé Langley and three other women.[3]

It is a constant thrill to discover these things, but frightening to be aware of how easily they could have been lost. All too often relatives and friends throw away important, useful and interesting documents after a person's death. This is particularly so with lesbian concerns and should serve as a constant reminder to us all that we are the keepers of our own lesbian history. We should never lose it or let it disappear. It is up to lesbians to be ever-vigilant in the preservation of our history. We can certainly be sure that no one else will preserve it for us.

So, when faced with all these potential hazards, just how did we manage to find all these older lesbians who were willing to publicly tell their stories? That search was not always easy, even though we have a lot of experience in discovering women's history and have been lesbians for a long time. We advertised; we found names in the *Arena 3* magazines and rifled through 'phone books to see if we could find them again – imagine the surprise at being 'phoned twenty-five years after you put in an ad. We talked to lots of people; wrote to organisations; went to meetings and simply approached anyone and everyone. One of the most difficult initial tasks is to persuade unknown people actually to give us their time and talk to us. Some women were prepared to talk to us, but not to appear on TV; others were willing to tell their stories on television, but not to be visible or recognisable; others felt able to be open and visible and obviously some just said frankly no!

We were determined from the start that the programme was to be their stories, not our fixed ideas and structures into which we would fit them. As always, our research was the starting point. We embark upon it without any preconceived ideas, so that the process becomes what we call 'organic'. Our method is to talk to as many people as possible and make sound recordings of these interviews. Every stage is painstakingly transcribed. These interviews help us to build up a picture of their experiences and lead us on to further research. Eventually, from all this we can work out the best way to represent these experiences on film. Obviously, our own political dimensions and lesbian/feminist perspectives come into play in this process.

We filmed a broad cross-section of women, and, whilst some always knew they were lesbians, others discovered it later in life, after they had married. They discussed dress, stereotypes and the complex issue of role-playing which also had a dramatic effect on the early lesbian meetings organised by *Arena 3* in 1964. They told us about love and romance, falling in love in middle age for the first time, the pressures that led some of them to marry; memories of London's Gateways Club; feminism, politics and Black women's issues; the late discovery, for some, of their lesbian identity and subsequent coming out to their children and friends; plus their hopes and philosophies for the future. The end result was a fifty-minute documentary featuring sixteen older lesbians and highlighting aspects of lesbian life this century.

In addition, we were left with hours of unused material which we wanted to make more widely available. This book includes the stories of fourteen women from the programme plus five others who, for various reasons, were not in the film. Their stories are edited from several interviews and include their amendments and some updates.

It is important to remember that the questions we asked were for a television programme and were not intended to be an exhaustive account of lesbian history, nor, indeed, the complete life stories of women we interviewed. These stories are moments in time of their fascinating lives and form a valuable part of our history.

These moving stories give a very personal insight into the joy and sadness of the lives of these women. All of them are both exceptional and ordinary.

19

NOTES

1. The Gateways *club*, or 'Gates' *as it was affectionately known, became the most famous lesbian club in London. It opened in the 1930s, a bohemian, arty-type club. Gradually, after the Second World War it became increasingly gay and predominantly lesbian. By the late 1960s it was exclusively lesbian. It was frequented by women from all over the world and featured in the renowned film* The Killing of Sister George *in 1969. It finally closed its doors in 1985. For most of that time, the* Gates *was run by Gina, initially with her husband, Ted, and then with her lesbian partner, Smithy.*

   The Gateways *is mentioned in the stories of Ceri Ager, Pat James, Pat G, Sharley McLean, Jackie Forster and Diana Chapman.*

2. *Clause 28 became law as Section 28 of the Local Government Act, 1988. It bans local councils, and any organisations and schools they support, from 'promoting homosexuality'.*

3. *In 1963, a group of five women, including Diana Chapman ana Esmé Langley, got together and formed a society called* The Minorities Research Group. *Its aim was to help lesbians with the difficulties of guilt, isolation and loneliness and encourage them to come to terms with themselves by providing a counselling service. Its first monthly newsletter,* Arena 3, *was produced in January 1964 and was the first all-lesbian publication. The magazine featured articles on the causes of lesbianism, lesbian relationships, the problems of living as a lesbian as well as how to put men off if they tried to pick you up! It aimed to improve the public image of lesbians and be honest and realistic. In addition,* Arena 3 *published more general material including poetry, short stories and book reviews. It also provided a forum for debate through the letters pages.*

After several months, subscribers asked for meetings and these took place monthly in the Shakespeare's Head in Carnaby St., London.

Arena 3 *finally closed in 1971 and some women went on to found* Sappho.

Arena 3 *features in the stories of Rachel Pinney, Ceri Ager, Jackie Forster, Diana Chapman and Rosanna Hibbert.*

RACHEL PINNEY

My life story is that my love, which is everybody's strongest emotion, has been labelled wrong from the earliest I can possibly remember. It's something that feels right to me inside, and always has, but society thinks it's wrong.

Lesbian is a dirty word. It's bracketed with slime, muck, the devil – all the other dirty words you can think of. It's been a bad word right up to recently. I even find it difficult to use now. I will use homosexual anytime, rather than lesbian. As a child, of course, I never knew it. My first introduction was *The Well Of Loneliness*, I think. Even then, Radclyffe Hall never used the word 'lesbian' – she talked about 'inverts'. And I didn't know what an invert was. So I think right till grown up age, I never knew what a lesbian was. And then when I did, it was something down there in the gutter. And – even vaguely realising that maybe I was one of them – it still was down there in the gutter.

The first time I ever went to bed with anyone – not sexual – I was at Bristol University, so I was about eighteen or nineteen. There were two people I went to bed with there – just went to bed. One of them Estelle, had had a girlfriend before me and said 'We parted'. I met her later, and she said, 'We parted because her feelings were getting like those of a man, and, therefore, we had to part.' I remember thinking

– remember I was eighteen in those days – I remember thinking 'Well, I've got around to going there now, and I've got around to staying the night there. I even get into bed with her – I'm sure there's something else that people do.' I know it's funny – you're laughing – but it wasn't funny then. I was really puzzled. I just couldn't think what it was. I didn't think of sex, but there was something sort of not quite . . what's the next thing? And I just didn't know. One night she said, 'You know, you're sleeping with me too often.' I was supposed to be in the hostel. So I went out and slept rough – I slept on the games field and caught a cold. But I didn't know anything about it. I wouldn't even have thought sexually. I don't think that I'd ever heard of an orgasm, I don't think I knew what it was.

The next thing I remember about Estelle was that I wrote her a letter saying I'm engaged to be married. And typically, Estelle was a terrifically sarcastic pen and tongue. She sent me a postcard with 'Congratulations' in the middle of it and that was all. It never occurred to me that she should feel anything about it at all. So you're now listening to the naïvety of the 1930s.

I got married as part of my effort to conform. I didn't conform very much – aristo family, landed gentry, – but I married a working class man, Italian, at that. My father would hardly look at him, but my mother went out of her way to be tolerant. Thinking of class, we had nothing in common at all, absolutely nothing except that he called himself a Communist in those days, and that was only skin deep. We had absolutely nothing in common, and so I married him. I wanted to have kids. So, that's all. It was not an important event in my life, except that I got three lovely children, and I think they'd be rather cross to hear me say that it was not an important event, but it wasn't.

I think I knew I might be a lesbian in the early days of the war. I had a kid of three – let's place ourselves at about 1943 – and I needed some babysitting. Somebody advertised, and she was one of the early lesbians of the gang in Chelsea in those days. I went to call on her, and talked about the advert and talked about the babysitting – she wanted a job so as to dodge the call-up. I don't think anything very much happened in the interview, except that we arranged the job. She told me later that when her girlfriend came home she said 'Cor! I've had such a big . . . '– and she used a slang word for lesbian, I don't know what it was – '. . . in here talking.' And I thought, 'How did she know? And am I?' So I said, 'Well, how did you know I was?' And she said, 'Well, it's all over you – the way you walk, the way you talk, look at your clothes, everything about you.' I said 'Oh, is it?' I felt really bad about it and never, ever thought of it as anything good. What I really felt was it was something awful like dirt, filth, slime – all the things that were bad. Then I got to know her, all her friends, all her gang.

My first sexual relationship with a woman was after the war in 1945. And it was a rather, non-U, sub-threshold gang that I sort of fraternised with occasionally – terrified that ever anyone should know. And I used to go to these lesbian parties absolutely in fear of death – no way would I let a *real* person know it or a *real* person see it. It was something sort of way out.

When I set up in medical practice in Chelsea I tried to be respectable – that was in 1949 – I put on lipstick and I wore a skirt, for the first six months until I got established. One of the things I was terrified of, was that any of them would turn up in the waiting room. So I put on respectability, for six months. And being respectable meant not fraternising with your lesbian friends.

I had a series of girlfriends, they were all either my secretary in the practice, or attached to the practice in some way or other. But no word would be spoken, and I denied it fiercely if anyone mentioned it. You've no idea how strong this thing was. Like if I'd committed murder, I wouldn't admit it, ever, to anybody. I thought 'Well, this is the way to behave.' You keep it absolutely to yourself as something you've got, like smelly feet. I have resisted the word lesbian, and I remember I had a girlfriend and no way was I allowed to say her name to anybody. This would have been approximately round about 1951 when I was forty-two. Her brother once said to me 'I'm really concerned because I understand you're a lesbian, and I do not like to see you close to my sister.' And I did exactly the same to him. I turned round and denied it fearfully. She denied it so strongly that to this day I'm not allowed to refer to her as anything except 'Anon'. I denied it and I swore at this man. But no way would I admit to being a lesbian. It was something that wasn't nice, and you didn't admit it, though I *do* admit I've been to prison.

Around 1963, I was beginning to get a little braver. And along comes Esmé (Langley)[1], knocks at my door while I'm in practice, she comes into the kitchen and chats around. And I said, 'Look, what are you really doing? Trying to start a lesbian organisation? Why have you come to me?' And then I said, 'Anyway, if something's going to be done, it shouldn't be done by somebody like you – dressed like that, looking like that.' I mean, she came in looking like an ordinary butch les, not all that butch. And she quoted this – that it was because she was so outraged at my response to her interview with me, that she started up the *Arena 3* magazine. I think Esmé is one of the people – there are a few in my life when you look back – whom I feel I short-changed very much. She was looking for help and she didn't get it from me. But she certainly was short-changed by me. I don't like people coming to the door asking for help and being given something else – it's not a nice way to live. But I was absolutely horrified that she didn't look like someone straight out of *Vogue*. If you're going to sell a thing like lesbian, you've got to look like *Vogue*.

I went to one of the first lesbian gatherings. I walked five times round the block and then didn't go in, you know. And then I met somebody else – we went into them terrified. There was a man then, Bryan Magee, who wrote a book called *One In Twenty* and he came to one of those meetings of *Arena 3*,[2] and hung around and interviewed people. He then wrote this book. Esmé went a bit nuts, saying that he gets the facts from us, writes a book and gets all the royalties – and she was very upset about it. He also wrote an article in the *New Statesman*, called "The Facts about Lesbianism". I showed it to a friend and she was pretty disgusted by it, and all he did was to list the three main classic positions.[3] This hit the headlines – you know, he wrote nothing about the 'oomph' of homosexuality. It shows how naïve the approach was – all everybody thought about was who does what with what and to whom. And this was an obsession right through my naïve days. It simply obsessed people – who did what with what and to whom.

Way back in 1973, I think, Dennis Mitchell interviewed me on my private life and put it out on Granada TV. I was answering all these questions, and then Dennis suddenly – out of the blue – said to me 'How long have you known you're a lesbian, Rachel?' And I blew a gasket, and when I blow a gasket, I *can*. I can sort of string all the four-letter words together in miles, I can't do it unless I'm revved up, but I said, 'You just put that bloody camera down the drain, or I'll come and smash the thing all to pieces! Cut that! And what the hell do you mean, asking me that?' You know. And I swore at him. And he said 'I'm sorry, Rachel, I didn't know you minded.' The point of that story is not that incident, but the date. The date was 1973.

Now I've got a fabulous girlfriend, Sally, I've got a wonderful girlfriend – I feel really good. And I've got to say a really big thank you to her for that. I feel really good, because Sally sat on a bus and held my hand. Never would I have dared to do that to anybody. Sally even once canoodled my leg in full public, in a station waiting room somewhere by the sea or something. I had shorts on. I mean it's unbelievable for anyone who's lived through my generation, that that could be allowed to happen. So, I'm really enjoying Sally's lack of inhibition.

Sally's openness about being homosexual with me is a source of daily joy. I mean, dammit, there's a bloody great big double bed, not much else in that room next door. So if she's not sleeping with me, who's she sleeping with? It's amazing, you know, it continues to amaze me. It's like anything else that you've achieved which you never thought you would. And I'm absolutely loving it, I'm loving taking Sally round and openly talking about her, openly having her as a partner without having to think that she's something else. I had to invent a name for a girlfriend I lived with longest – she's dead now. I made her my student-assistant so that she had an excuse for being around, and she became a medical student in my practice. But I had to invent a name for her.

Now that Sally and I have been together for five years, we're beginning to run into real trouble. We're beginning to find that our real differences, and there are real things that we can't take in the other one, are beginning to be the cause of rows. In fact, we can express anger to each other. I said the other day – and meant it – twice running, 'I hate you, I hate you', and put a pretend strangle round her neck. It was true at the time. And that was a wonderful moment for me, because it was true at the time. But it's not true, I'm attached to someone I want to go on living with and now we've got to dig in and work at it. The other day she wrote down a list of sixty three things she didn't like about me. I wasn't supposed to see them, but I did, eventually. They slot into very good categories of things one can't change. You know, this is me, and I'm not going to change. Things I won't change, because I think they're all right and I don't want to change them. Things that are mistakes, mistakes in communications, and just petty little personal irritations that everybody has. Why the hell have we waited five years before doing it? In other words, in those early days of being in love, you can begin to really take on where the other guy's different. You can do it. But one doesn't spend one's spare time doing any talking about the real things. And that's a pity, because, of course, they're there, of course there are differences. And of course we're going through them now. We actually are tottering on the borderline now. We could break and we could not, and I don't think either of us want to break.

But we did in February 1990.

I think we split up because Sally saw that we were strangling each other long before I did, and what she needed I couldn't give her, and what I needed she couldn't give me. She saw that we were destroying each other. I mean she was sabotaging my work and I was sabotaging her way of life. One of her sixty-three things was that I didn't take an interest in her work. I DID! I thought I did, I always followed her interviews and where she went and backed them up and everything, but we were destroying each other's work. See, my work is very intuitive in a Rachel sort of way, and her work is very establishment in a Sally sort of way. She was destroying my work, she thought I was taking too many workshops and suddenly scotched them, just like that, without any warning and I went beserk! Whereas I was increasing them! Do you see? Because I was doing them well, I thought, and wanting more of them, she wanted less of them, so we *were* destroying each other's work, our work means a lot to both of us.

Sally and I were absolutely adept at trying to give the other person what they wanted, both in bed and out. We were absolutely skilled at getting it dead wrong every time. We tried. Sally saw it, I didn't. She described the last year together as trying to patch up a dying relationship. With tremendous skill and expense she laid on three events – as something that would be the nicest possible thing for me and got it absolutely dead wrong. That's what we were doing and this is what you do when you try and merge two people. The lesson I've learnt is you don't merge, you've got to be yourself. I think it's a piece of pathology in our culture, that when you fall 'in love', whatever that may mean, you fall into this merging. Well, you're NOT the other person, you're yourself. And what you do when you fall in love is you lose yourself in the other person, you attempt a merger. We were trying to please each other, do you see? I was trying to please her and give her what she wanted. She didn't want me to give her what she wanted, she wanted me to WANT to give her what she wanted. She wanted me to WANT it too, and you can't be what you're not.

When Sally wrote the sixty-three things she didn't like about Rachel, my first reaction was how can I change every one of these things to please Sally, and I was shaken by that. So I thought that those sixty-three things should be done at the beginning of the honeymoon, not at the end. Have these sixty-three things out early. That I think is important. To deal with these difficulties then, and be able to say, these things I am willing to change, I think they are bad habits, and these are things that I don't think should be changed – they're part of me and my lifestyle and they're not going to alter. Things that the other person doesn't like. Now if there's something that the other person just doesn't like that's part of you, either you've got to change or they've got to put up with it. Then you've just got to accept that. But when we actually did split up, the very FIRST thing I learnt was that it is NOT love that first panic, that first agony is not love, it is panic at losing the person that's there. It was panic at being left. It was panic at somebody not being there. A piece of news you want to come in and tell the person: 'Oh, I must tell so and so that', and they're not there to be told. There's not another person that you can lean over and stroke the buttock of in the middle of the night. The other person isn't THERE, just isn't there, and you long to write them a letter, you want to tell them things. You learn to share everything – well you can't share EVERYTHING. Some things you can't share and I think it was a pity, in a way, that our work was so close, because although it was so close, we were so different. My working partner said if Sally hadn't known that you'd be all right, I don't think she'd have left you. Well she's a caring person, she knew I could take care of myself with a lot of support, she knew I had a strong support group. So, I had the panic, and then was a BLOODY nuisance to all my support group and friends and I made a rule that nobody was to let me grumble. I've spent a long time during the last forty weeks, splitting it all up into bits and it took right up 'til now. Yesterday was breakthrough day. I suddenly realised that I could live without her. I could live without a partner and that was marvellous. I now only mention her about once a day instead of once every half hour, so, she is not dominant in my thinking. The door will open and I'm not thinking it's Sally coming through it the whole time.

People are there – I'm not alone, I'm not, I was lonely in the evening, I'm not lonely in the evening any longer. Slowly I've just slipped back into myself, I don't know how I did it. I worked, I worked a lot, saw a lot of people, didn't shut up, didn't shut up to anybody, even people in my workshops knew I was in trouble. And now I love her. I just love her. I mean she's Sally, if she walked through that door I'd be delighted to see her.

She WANTS to stay friends and so do I and that's what it's all about, isn't it? Well that's part of what it's all about. I mean I have lived through the pain. I think that's the motto, live through the pain. You don't stop loving just because they've left you, that's the message. The message is that the love is still there, whatever love is, and I love Sally. She'll have a welcome here any time she comes, she'll have a bed like anyone else here if she wants to, but I'm not going to live with her. I'm not going to live with her in my environment. I might visit her in hers, she might visit me in mine, but I'm not going to coalesce any longer. I still love her; you can't stop loving. I don't hate her, there's nothing to hate about her and I think this final thing she did was magnificent, to have the courage to do it. She had the courage to break – to give up a home, which means a lot to her, and to give up her job. I just have nothing but admiration for it, and she did it. I doubt if I would've done it. I have a lot of courage, I thought I was the one that had courage, but it looks as though she is. I mean she's got it, and give her my love! Tell her I'm all right will you? Yes, tell her I'm being myself!

NOTES

1. *Esmé Langley was one of the five founders of the Minorities Research Group in 1963 who went on to produce the newsletter Arena 3. Esmé had probably heard of Rachel's lesbianism through the Chelsea lesbian set even though Rachel herself was very closeted at this time.*

2. *See note 3 after the introduction.*

3. New Statesman, 26 March 1965. *'The Facts About Lesbianism –A Special Inquiry into a Neglected Problem' The three 'commonplace techniques of lesbian intercourse' he lists are tribadism, mutual masturbation and cunnilingus.*

ELEANOR

      I knew I was a lesbian when I was fourteen. I accepted it as natural. It was natural to me that I loved women – I was never interested in boys, men, it was always women. When I was fourteen, I left elementary school, and went to a Women's Evening Institute. It was a club, we were all women together, did everything together – holidays, swimming, netball. I was in a netball team and went all over London playing. We spent holidays together – we were in the atmosphere of caring for women – in gym classes, etc. A lot of us had crushes on other women and a lot of us have never married. Four of us quickly formed an exclusive group. We were all lesbians and there were many more we were aware of among the wider group of students. We four did everything together and even broke the ice at the Women's Pond at Highgate one New Year's Day.

      I never felt like I was the only one. I had an Eton crop and I used to wear a collar and tie, though not for work, obviously. I was always a bit that way inclined. I was young and brash at the time, and I didn't care what I did. We thought we were the cat's whiskers. We wore French berets when they first came over to England. We were a group of women who were really lesbians, although we didn't use that term, we knew what the word meant and had used it. We never felt that we had to follow society. We were quite different, I don't know how to explain it, but I've never grown up with the feeling that I had to do this, or I had to do that – get married or whatever. Because my parents died when I was quite young, I was a free agent. At sixteen, I had my first woman lover, we rented rooms and lived together for five years.

We were all dying to get hold of *The Well Of Loneliness* and we passed it round even when it was banned. It was quite dog-eared. We just thought it was wonderful, because we knew we were like that. As I said, we didn't use the word lesbian but we knew we loved women. To find a book like that was absolutely marvellous. It was as near as one could get to reading about women who loved each other. I moved among women that were of my persuasion, but we were all alike. So I hardly ever went about with people who weren't lesbians. My life was caught up with them. And we just grew up, like that, until I applied to the London County Council (LCC), as it was then, for a scholarship to go on the land. In 1937 I went to agricultural college for a year and was a dairy and poultry maid on a farm in Suffolk where I met my next woman lover. And that was a different matter, because then we did have to dress like men – jodphurs, mainly, because that was the only thing you could get for farm work. I wore them, all the time. I had to. Of course, my lover lived with me, but I don't think the owners of the farm thought anything of it. They didn't say. I don't suppose we cared, really. We lived our own life together for five years until unforeseen circumstances forced us to part, but we remained friends.

I've had a wonderful life and always been able to meet women. I think my lesbianism was more hidden when I came off the land and went into the Civil Service in 1947. Then I had to be very, very careful and I've been careful ever since. It was not long before I met my third lover, we rented a flat in Chelsea and were together for five years before we parted. She had found another woman and this time I was devastated. A few months later, I met Doreen at work in 1952 when I was teaching in the Civil Service and we were attracted to each other. We used to go out together every lunch time, and gradually we fell in love. We lived together for thirty long and loving years until she died, and we were very happy. Towards the end of her life she became very ill, this was a very anxious time for us and as she got worse it became harder to maintain the old feelings for each other. She was ill for two years, I used to pick her up from the hospital on Saturday mornings and take her back on Sunday evenings so that she had some sort of home life from the hospital. I knew she would have done that for me. As we were both Christians, you might say Christian lesbians, I always felt that whatever I was, I was as God made me and her. I used to take her to church on Sunday mornings, no matter how erratic her behaviour was at times.

We never hid the fact that we were fond of each other. We were always together and I was with her when she died. She did know me, she just opened her eyes once, and I kissed her goodbye. I felt I couldn't express my grief openly because, to other people, it was only the sadness of losing a friend. It suddenly hit me, about eighteen months to two years afterwards, that I was alone. I was bereft of joy, you might say. I felt there had to be more to life. So I wrote to this newly formed committee that I had read about in the paper. The GLC Women's Committee. They sent me the bulletin of the Older Lesbian Network. And I attended my first OLN meeting in April 1985.

For the first three times, I had to have someone to go with. I was nervous about meeting all these new women. But I've never been sorry that I got in touch with them, because it made a terrific difference to my life. I've made quite a few good friends there and it's been a life-saver.

I wouldn't want to come out now, at my age, because it would involve maybe a breaking up of some relationships with friends, and family. You get into a habit of not talking about it. After meeting Doreen, we didn't noise it abroad – I expect people thought of us as friends but I know some people wouldn't understand. I look back with anguish and joy to the wonderful years I spent with her –

35

anguish that her illness was so terrible and final; and joy because of her love for me. I know that in the hereafter we shall meet again as we will with all our loved ones.

CERI AGER

When I was sixteen, I had a crush on the head girl at school, Jo-Jo, who left two years before me. We still saw each other – and used to go out together to theatres and parties. Until I was eighteen, she never said a word to me about lesbianism. Then, she asked me why I hadn't got any boyfriends. I told her that I didn't like boyfriends, didn't like boys, I liked going out with her. I asked if she didn't like going out with me. And she said, 'Oh yes, I just wanted to know if you had any boyfriends.' And then she said, 'Do you know why you haven't got any boyfriends, why you don't like them?' I said, 'No, I just *don't like them*.' And then very sweetly and very nicely, she explained it all to me. I just gave her a great big hug and kiss and said, 'Well, that's wonderful!'

I just knew that she was absolutely the person that I was terribly, terribly fond of, and her explanation fitted in with how I knew I felt. It grew from there and we met her other friends – who welcomed my coming out so naturally.

I was very happy, I felt contented. I didn't feel nervous. My mother didn't know, she was really very, very innocent. Jo-Jo would stay with me at weekends, and my mother used to say 'Oh, how awfully nice that your school friend will come and stay with you over the weekends, you're an only one and it's right for you to have company', which rather tickled us. But my father knew. He never said anything about it, but I knew by the twinkle in his eye when Jo-Jo was around. I was so lucky, I didn't have any sort of hassle or embarrassment. There was no interference from the media, nothing on radio, there wasn't even television, then. And life went on beautifully. Then they thought my mother was dying. The doctor swore she wasn't going to get better. And my mother said, 'You are the only one. I can't die, you're not married. I am so worried about you.' And everybody – the bank manager, the local vicar, our solicitor, everybody, got at me, to get married. 'You should let your mother die happy.' I didn't want to get married, but I'd had one or two proposals. And when she was terribly, terribly ill and we really thought it was the end, I accepted one of these proposals and I got married. My mother lived till she was 76, and highly regretted what had happened. Within a year, I walked out on my husband. Jo-Jo was so understanding about it. It hurt us both, but we stayed together for ten years until she was killed the year before the war ended.

When Jo-Jo died, I went mad. For two or three months I wouldn't see anybody. I just sat alone, utterly, utterly miserable. Then I went to parties and parties, drinking far too much, one night here and one night there, and a week here and a week there with any woman who attracted me, until I calmed down. Really, it was just getting over the shock of losing Jo-Jo.

Then I started travelling, spending a year here and a year there and what have you. I was rather like the sailors – I had a girlfriend in every port. I had an Egyptian/Russian girlfriend in Egypt for two or three years whose sister lived in France, and decided it was time she got married and came and literally dragged her out of Egypt. I got this pathetic letter from the outskirts of Paris, saying her sister was busy getting her engaged and she'd let me know when the awful day came. I never heard from her again. Then I decided if I wanted even a state pension, I'd better work for a while and stay put.

I didn't like clubs. I went once or twice to the Gateways.[1] I remember the first time I went there – it must have been almost when it first opened. I couldn't believe it. There was a three-piece orchestra – a pianist and a violinist and somebody else – playing in the corner quietly, and all the pairs sitting sedately about. This was an awful long time ago – I must have been in my late twenties when it first started, about forty-odd years ago. It was lovely, very role-conscious: one person feminine and sweet, and one person with tie and suit. Afternoon tea and coffee, then it went on to drinks in the evening and dancing. Then I didn't go for a long while. When I came back, in the seventies it was frenetic. It was absolutely crazy then. There was very little role-playing then. Oh, it was great fun, everybody sort of knew everybody else and Phyllis behind the bar was great. To the world in general, it was a very wicked place to go, though! If you went to the Gateways, it was the Gateways of Hell.

In the sixties, I heard about MRG (Minorities Research Group) and *Arena 3*[2], and I thought, 'Oh, I'd like to do something with this,' because I had met people who were on the verge and frightened to come out. I knew how upset they were and I thought perhaps I'd be able to help a bit. Then the letters started coming in. Loads and loads of letters, some with money in – quite a few people sent us money. The letters had to be answered, and that seemed to be what I did, an awful lot of answering letters, and an awful lot of sitting and having people weep on my shoulder, listening to their stories. There were those who came from small villages and small towns who really thought they were the only ones, that there was nobody like them and that there was something wrong with them. They were thoroughly delighted when they knew there were hundreds of other people in the world like them. There were those who had found out that they were lesbians and they were deeply ashamed of it, and thought it was wrong. They wouldn't accept it – you had to work and work and talk to them to make them accept it. There were those who were suicidal about it. There were those who were thrilled to bits – thought it was absolutely marvellous, and what could they do? They were bursting to do something to help. There were those who were married and hadn't found out until then. It was very sad – they had children – and wanted to leave their husbands but could not, or would not, because of the children – they were very sad cases. Every day somebody came. And the letters, – there were stacks of letters. And then we had to get the magazine out on a horrible old duplicator that was always going wrong.

I'll tell you a funny thing. When people were very, very down, there was a pub just round the corner, and I used to take them there and buy them a double brandy to cheer them up. One night, I'd been working till about half past ten, I staggered into the pub before it closed, and said, 'I want two double brandies.' The bloke behind the bar said, 'Have them on the house, love. How do you pull all these lovely women?' And I replied, 'Well, how do you think?' And he gave me an old fashioned look, and said, 'Ahh. Mmm.' I'll always remember that.

Some of the younger ones were quite happy about things. They used to pay their £2 sub and say, 'Would you like to come to the pictures tonight?' I had to say 'No, I don't come in with the subscription.' They'd laugh and that would be it. But it was the older ones – women from thirty-five, forty onwards – who really were shocked, really were sad, and then they were very, very relieved when they found they weren't the only ones. We then started having meetings upstairs in a pub, once a month, and got some interesting people to talk to us and it sort of went on from there.

The club wasn't very big at first, and then, gradually, the pub used to get full upstairs. But we did use to get nasty remarks. Once it got known, that it *was* lesbians who were going upstairs, as you went past the bar, you'd get some nasty remarks from the men there. The thing to do was to sort of sweep by with your nose in the air, and pop upstairs.

There was a big debate in the meetings about wearing masculine attire.[3] I didn't like suits and collars and ties – slacks and sweaters,

40

yes, but I didn't like it when they went to absolute extremes. It was their business, but I didn't like it myself. I didn't like it because it made the 'normal' person uncomfortable and it put them against lesbians. I found – I think it was the beginning of coming out – the more masculine ones wanted to show the world by dressing. Really it was a great shame, because it did antagonise an awful lot of people.

After a while, I went abroad again, and when I came back, they'd altered the whole format. And, *Sappho*⁴ started up. The people who had been with us from the beginning, quite a lot of them, went over to *Sappho*. And Jackie Forster was working from a basement off the Edgware Road, behind Marble Arch. I used to go down there on a Saturday and help her.

I've always been independent and found that young people have been attracted to me. That has always worried me. Several affairs that I was really happy with I ended because I was over twenty years older. They seemed so stable, but I thought, 'Well, what's going to happen? When they're forty I shall be sixty, when they're fifty, still on the go, I shall be seventy-odd and somebody's going to get hurt, so it's better that I hurt them now by breaking it off than hurting each other later on when I'm older. I don't know why I didn't attract anybody my own age. My last really serious lover, Ricky, was ten years younger than me. But she was very sensible, and we seemed more on a par. She saw an advertisement for *Arena 3*, and wrote to us. She read a lot and I read a lot and she quoted from lots of books and she wrote reams of letters. So I wrote back and we agreed to meet. I was going abroad that summer. But I thought, 'No, I'll go to Wales to see her instead.' She'd had a ghastly time, it was awful. She had also got married under pressure. Her husband left her and married his secretary. She tried to commit suicide. Somebody went in with a book they'd borrowed or something and caught her just in time. Then she went to live in Wales in a tiny little village, in a tiny little cottage with her young daughter, who was only ten. We got on very well together and I stayed for my holiday with her and I went back at weekends. Finally, they joined me in my London flat. And that relationship lasted for ten years until Ricky died of cancer.

The April after the February that she died, I went into hospital. In the meantime, my legs were like tree trunks, but I used to be able to waddle around. Then I was back in hospital and I've been disabled ever since. A year after being disabled I regained my independence. And I thought to myself, 'No, I don't want to get up in the morning and get someone's breakfast, have a meal ready at night. I want to eat when I want to eat, go out when I want to go out and stay in bed all day sometimes.' You get very selfish when you're living alone.

Now I'm pretty busy – I'm on four or five management committees which include an active pensioners' organisation and I do voluntary work at the London Lighthouse.[5] I visit my friends and they visit me. I really don't seem to have much time to spare, which is lovely. Though sometimes I find I've got a day off, and I think 'Oh! I've got a whole day to myself this week.' And I just flop and read, doing absolutely nothing. But I couldn't stay in all the time. I just could not sit and do nothing feeling sorry for myself. The time will come when I'll have to, I suppose, but I hope it won't be for a while.

I think things are much, much easier for lesbians now. We have lesbian clubs, and we've got the *Pink Paper*[6], various magazines and lots more books by lesbian writers. Also, look at the numbers that came on the Gay Pride march in 1989. There were literally thousands. And they knew they'd be likely to be shown on television or in the newspaper. A few years ago, you wouldn't have got that many people to show themselves. Though you still, of course, do get those that are frightened to come out and for them it isn't easy.

I don't mind people knowing. If you're a lesbian you're a lesbian, and if you're a true lesbian, you really shouldn't mind other people knowing. I think you should always stand up for your sisters.

NOTES

1. *See Note 1 of the introduction.*
2. *See Note 3 of the introduction.*
3. *This debate is also told in Diana Chapman's story.*
4. *See Note 4 after Jackie Forster's story.*
5. *London Lighthouse is a hospice and a counselling and drop-in centre for people with AIDS or who have been diagnosed HIV positive.*
6. *A free weekly paper produced in London by lesbians and gay men.*

ELLEN

Well, my mother was a dancer. And I just danced before I could walk, so I'm told. It was all I ever wanted to do. When I was twelve I joined a kiddies' troop, and went on from there. One of the twelve rosebuds, or you know, Beam's Breezy Babes. I was a Beam's Breezy Babe. It was lovely.

I've been in the theatre all my life. When I was first on tour, there was a girl, Edna, I was very keen on her, and she rather liked me so – I thought, 'This is it.' I'd always preferred women's company, but not really in a sexual way, I thought it wasn't, you know, 'nice'. I just liked women and it seemed natural to me. But when I met Edna I just knew that's what I wanted to be, that's what I wanted to do.

Then I went to Paris with a show, and I met an English girl there – she's dead now I'm afraid, all dead, dear – called Nancy Wallace, who was very well known in the clubs, and she was the one who took me to the place called the Coffee Ann[1] in London. It was most famous, and from there I met loads of people. I went to a club in Gerrard Street, and it was 42 Gerrard Street, and called The 42nd. It was probably about the time of '42nd Street'. And all the girls used to gather there, night after night. This is where I met Marion – "Billy". She lived in Croydon, and was a secretary in quite a well-known furniture company. I used to stay with her, but I was mostly on tour. I

45

was her girlfriend – I was about eighteen or nineteen, and Billy was much older – about twenty years older than me.

To me, I was just going to be a star then. I never was, but everyone knows that I was *the* tap dancer in the West End then, and I always thought I'd make the star billing. So Billy and I did have a close relationship, but I didn't want to settle down for life. She was such a nice person, and she was very interested in Russia, and used to sell the *Daily Worker*[2] on the corner by the Town Hall. So although my life was always dancing, hers was . . . she always wanted to go to Russia, and she used to write reams about it and go to meetings. So we really led our own lives. She was very butch, a very, very butch lady. Very serious. She was what I would call today a company secretary. She always dressed in a suit – and beautifully – she used to have her suits made. And always had a collar and tie, different ties, and very, very cropped hair. My mother accepted her, but people didn't ask about her, she was just my friend, you see. They didn't go into the physical side of it – and I don't think they wanted to know, or my mother didn't. My sisters were so 'normal' – hah, that word again. They didn't understand it – 'Oh, a funny girlfriend our sister's got, you know, or woman friend.' But for so many girls then – or women – that was their clothing. Collar and ties. Billy was really lovely. I did love her very much, very much indeed. She was a very sweet person. She loved the theatre, and she loved to watch me dance. But at forty-two or three, she became ill with what we thought was sort of early menopause, and so did the doctor, – she was fainting and so on. And she became ill with pernicious anaemia. Within a couple of weeks, she had died. So that was very sad, and a great loss to me, and I took a long time to get over it.

At that time I was with *ENSA*[3], with Arthur Askey and that lot. I just went from show to show. I can't remember all the girlfriends I had. None of them were anybody I wanted to settle down with. I can't explain to you – you may think I'm odd, but I was only interested in the theatre. But sexually, I preferred women to men and nobody ever thought to ask me why. We didn't discuss things like that – like 'Why haven't you got married?' really. Well, in our family we didn't.

My mother loved the gay boys, and they loved her. They'd take her down the clubs. My other two sisters were very naïve – they didn't know what sort of clubs they were. There was the Robin Hood in Bayswater. But you had a circle of friends, and went to different houses. We used to go to the 'Lily Pond' – on the first floor of the Coventry Street Corner House at Piccadilly Circus, named because all the 'boys' used to go for afternoon tea on a Sunday, and then the 'girls' started to get in – it was well known. It was a sight to come and see in London, the 'Lily Pond' on a Sunday afternoon. We'd all meet there in our Sunday best. The girls were very butch. The butch ones were butch. From there, we'd go back to someone's flat. And there was Bina – she was the first Black lesbian and friends with everyone. Very nice looking girl. Then we'd go off to one of the clubs. That was a thing you all did. All the queers got together. But you all kept together, you had no outsiders, 'straight' is what you say today, we used to call it normal in those days, you know. You were either queer or normal. If one of the normals was interested, you knew that he or she had potential. Otherwise, you didn't have anybody's sisters, you know, or anybody hanging on. The social life was marvellous.

I went from show to show, girlfriend to girlfriend, until I met Ena, now dead. It's awful, you feel so old when you say 'now dead'. She lived in Hampstead. I don't know whether I was madly in love with her, but she was another one who was as nice to me as Billy was. She was nice. I always went for someone who could teach me something, because I knew I didn't have much schooling. You see, I left school at twelve. Although I did actually win a scholarship to go to the Brompton Oratory; but I never went, because I was mad to go on the stage, and my teacher said 'She is a dancer born.'

Ena was another very butch-looking number, very handsome really. Had a mop of lovely grey hair – it went grey when she was very young. Of course, she used to pick up girls, you see, all the time. I didn't actually live with her then, I was on tour quite a lot, and earning good money. I was a leading dancer in many shows, and had to support my mother. I used to go and stay with Ena for days on end, or we'd go to Brighton. A lot of the girls seemed to be down in Brighton. There were many pubs in Brighton, like the Clarence. Ena used to go down there with this girl or that girl. I was very hurt by it all, but she always said I was 'the one', and I was a bit simple, I thought I was, very trusting I was.

I had a chance to go to South Africa with an Ivor Novello show – we used to call it a tour of 'Dancing Queers'. When I was there I met this fellow, John, my late husband. I didn't really dislike men. I'd just never thought about them and I didn't want to go to bed with them. If I wanted to go to bed with anyone, it would be with a girl or a woman. But John was very kind to me, and was a real gentlemen. He was a widower with two little girls and, before I left, he asked me to marry him. I said, 'Ooh, no. I'm not the marrying kind.' You couldn't say 'I'm ... you know ...,' especially not in South Africa in those days.

I had to come back with the show, because you didn't run out on your contract, and we corresponded. I came back to Ena, and she said she was going to be ... you know, it was only me she ever wanted, and so on. And we had a great honeymoon. Then, of course, she started again, after we settled down again. I was still corresponding with this chap, and his family. He got more and more persistent, and I wrote and said I didn't love him, and wouldn't make any sort of a wife. He said he'd pay my fare to go back, – he was a very nice man, I liked him ever so much, very kind – he was like my brother. His sister was a lovely person. And he asked me to marry him again. So I thought, well, I think I will try this, I think I will have a go at normality, so I went back to South Africa and married. Of course, I'd never had anything whatever to do with a man, in the physical sense, you know, and from the very first night I knew I had made a terrible mistake. And I hated it, hated every minute of it, hated sexual intercourse with a man. I did all I could to get out of my marital duties, and then I became pregnant because I didn't know anything about contraception. When I became pregnant, I just became mentally ill, and wanted to go home and get away. I couldn't tell the doctor that I'd made an awful mistake – that I didn't like men, I liked women – but I did tell him I hated the physical side. He understood and said I must go home. He said my mental state was such that if I didn't go home not only would I lose the child, which didn't worry me if I did – I'm very glad now that I didn't – I would go off my rocker. So I came home. And that was the end of a beautiful friendship.

When I came home, who should be waiting for me at the dockside but Ena? And from then on she took care of me – right through my awful pregnancy. And that was it, and my daughter was born. And then I went to live with her. Ena was quite faithful for a while. Then she started all over again – women phoning up . . .

NOTES

1. *See description of Coffee Ann in Pat James' story.*

2. *Former name of the Communist Party daily newspaper, now entitled the* Morning Star.

3. *Entertainments for the Armed Forces during the Second World War.*

VICK ROBSON

When I was about fourteen, I answered this advert in the *Sunderland Echo* for a job down in Stanmore, Middlesex. They wanted a Cook General. My mam had to pawn her engagement ring so I could get my uniform, you know. I travelled twelve hours on the train. When I got there I was taught how to say things – 'Madam' not 'Missus', 'Sir' not 'Mister' and 'Master Steven' when the baby was born. I was the nanny and the lot.

I met this girl – she said 'I'm called Brenda and I come from Bermondsey.' I had a Saturday off once a month, and we used to go to London on a tuppence ticket for all round London. We became great mates, you know, and she says 'I wonder if you feel the same as I do?' I said 'I think so.' I was going to stick in at the YWCA, but she said she'd got a mate who'd got her own flat in Bermondsey where I could stay. It was there I had my first relationship with a woman, and it was wonderful. I'd never had a relationship with a man either then. We used to get on so well together. We had complimentary tickets, and we used to go to all the shows; joined the Wembley Lions Speedway Club. Our relationship was great, absolutely fantastic. And it was like equality between us, giving, you know, and that was good. And I thought 'What's this all about?' Wonderful! I felt so different then. We were together for about three years on and

51

off. It was then I knew I'd met the people that I could relate to, you know.

We used to discuss everything about lesbianism, what friends we had or hadn't, what it felt like to be up North, you know, locked in a pit village, not able to come out. Frustrating, all this. And we did get close, you know. Not too close, 'cos in those days, it just wasn't ... you know what I mean, the 1930s, I mean, that's a long time back.

We got on great, but when 1939 came and the war, my 'Missus' said 'You'll have to go back home, up North, because the war's started.' They were moving to Walton-on-Thames because my boss was something to do with the River Police. So I had to say goodbye to all the girls and oh, I was going to miss them! They said, 'What are you going to do next?' and I said 'Get away from where I'm going to live, 'cos it's horrible, closed in.' So I went back up North and I worked in this factory for about three months and it was three shifts and I still couldn't connect with the girls there. I had a Saturday night off and I went and signed myself up for the Air Force because I fancied that. I was nearly nineteen then.

We had a fortnight down in Gloucester doing our training and then we had to go to Morecambe to do our square bashing, you know. I was sent up to Long Benton, which was a barrage balloon place and I was there three months when it folded up. So I said, 'Oh, I'd like to be a driver', but they said, 'You're too short!' so I said, 'Oh, I'll be an electrician'. We were sent to Ullsworth to do a bit of training on some naval aircraft, stripping them down, you know, and building them up. I got in with some girls stationed there, and they said 'Are you like us?' So it started off again and I thought 'Oh, I'm back on Cloud Nine again.' Then I was sent up to Scotland; we went to do our training for seven months as an electrician and we all passed out as first-class air women.

Then I met Sheila – I was a corporal by then, and I had twenty-six girls in my flight, all electricians, you know. We were the first WAAF electricians, on aircraft engines, and they were glad to get us because all the laddies had to go abroad. I mean, we looked no different from anybody else, that's the thing. They'd say 'You don't look like a lesbian' – 'What do you mean, look like a lesbian? What do we do, walk round with a banner saying "I am a lesbian", and all this?' But it was knotted up inside you, then, you couldn't come out with it openly, but you felt it.

When I was stationed up in Scotland, I'd been there about a year and I was in the corporals' NAAFI. I was having coffee and it was really freezing, and this girl walked in, stripes on, you know, blonde, and I said, 'Oh, what are you doing here?' She says, 'Oh, I don't want to stop in this place, it's horrible!' 'Oh,' I says, 'Yeah? Come and have a coffee with me.' And they were playing 'In The Mood'. So we had a dance round together. That was our favourite tune – played by Joe Loss – at the time, you know. And I says 'You'll be all right here, I'll look after you.' So we really got on well together. We always met, you know, had a good laugh, we were really close.

She was engaged to this lad, a pilot, and they hadn't seen each other for a long while. She used to be one for going out at night and I used to leave my little window open in my bedroom. If she was out late, she'd knock on the window and say 'Vicky, can I come in? It's freezing outside.' I had me own little room, you see, at the top of the billet where all the other girls were. And I says 'Aye, come on in.' And she was always freezing. I was always warm, because I always kept myself fit, you see. So she used to cuddle in, and that was when we really got close, you know.

We ended up as good friends, really good friends. She was a corporal, signals, and I was a corporal electrician then, working on fighters and bombers. Interesting life, you got closer then you see. We used to go out together, dancing, and having a good time together – walks, whatever. And a sneaky little bit now and again! We really became close, you know, for three years. I said, 'You're not going back to that man, are you?' 'I have to,' she replied, and I said, 'Don't go.' And at the time she had to leave and go and get married to him.

When she had to go and catch the train back, I said 'Don't go' and we was crying in each other's arms. It was awful. And when she left, I sort of just went hollow, you know. And we wrote to each other. She always put at the end of the letter, 'Still love you.' You know. 'I still loves you.'

There must have been a hell of a lot of lesbians way back, you know, who couldn't come out on account of their families. It was that way with me. No friends around the same as yourself. So you had to bottle it all up, didn't you? What you'd call locked in the closet.

After the war finished – I came back up North again – my mother said, 'Now you're going to settle down, get married, have kids,' which I didn't want. I'd never been with a guy anyway. And I wasn't married till I was twenty-eight. So, I didn't like it one little bit. But I said I'm going to have two kids out of this. He wasn't really interested in the children at all, so I had to be a mam and dad to them both. Then, after about twelve years, I left him. I went to stay with me mother. She broke her hip. So I had to look after her – work shifts to get a new home together. Course, you couldn't get a house like you can now, if you leave. And me mam had just lost me dad. So I went to stay with me mother for two and a half years, and got a three-bedroomed house, which I had to start all over, working again – shift work getting good money. So I was able to pay for furniture and carpets.

When I moved over here a few years ago, and got my flat here in Newcastle, I 'phoned Lesbian Line, and I said, 'I want to come out – where's the nearest gay pub because I feel lost here?' She said, 'Do you want me to take you there?' and I said, 'No, I've got to do it by myself, because I want to make friends and come out, really come out. It's been forty years now I've been in the bloody closet.' It took me three nights to walk round, three afternoons to walk round and say 'I'm going in now.' I walked in and these girls are sitting beside me and they said 'Do you know this is a gay pub?' And I said, 'I wouldn't be sitting here if it wasn't, would I? All by myself.' And they invited me to sit with them. I was coming out again after forty years, because I felt I wanted to. I felt closed up and I'd locked it up for so long. It was tearing me apart. And the second day I walked in, the barmaid said, 'How do you feel now?' I says, 'Great.' So that's when I came out and I've been going there ever since – I feel I'm part of a family.

I've got me own place now, a flat. I'm really comfortable now. I do a morning paper round and I enjoy doing that, 'cos it's got me into the area, got me in the community, you know. So I've got friends all around me. I go running, been running for about fourteen years, and I work out at Ron's gym. I do a lot of reading to relax and I love dancing. Life is good for me now. I don't feel any of my age whatsoever. I can walk in any of those bars and be made welcome. And that's the way I feel about it. Really good. I just want to talk about it now, and bring it out. It helps those that's been on the marches, the demonstrations against the Clause 28.[1] And you can't push us back in the closet, because we're coming out on our own anyway. And that's what it's all about, isn't it?

NOTES

1. See Note 2 after the introduction.

PAT JAMES

When I was about eight, round about that age, I had a little friend staying the night and when I tried to cuddle her she moved away from me. I remember thinking she could go no further than the wall, so I followed her, and then she said 'If you don't stop it, I'm going to tell my mummy.' So that was the end of that, naturally. That was the first little incident, I suppose that gives an inkling of my feelings.

Then I remember when I was about thirteen, I had a another friend staying and we sort of got together and that was very natural. We just didn't talk about it even. I won't use the words 'made love' because we were experimenting I suppose, at that age. So that was my next experience. I was like a fish, I took to it like a fish to water. I didn't even question what was happening, I didn't feel different, didn't think of it. I wasn't very keen on boys anyway. I thought they were rather stupid . . . they didn't interest me at all. In fact, my opinion of males wasn't very high, though I was called a 'tomboy' like many an active young child, I suppose. Also I liked to play football and my father taught me how to box.

Then the war came when I was seventeen. I joined the ambulance service. I met a woman – my father didn't have a clue. My mother neither because she left when I was thirteen. So at seventeen, I was driving an ambulance, and I had to go to dinner one night with friends. There was a woman there, an artist's model, one of the notorious Augustus John's. When we were leaving, she said 'I'll drop you home.' I said yes, and we caught a taxi. The taxi had to turn round in the road and I fell over and ended up in her arms, it sounds incredible but she started kissing me. And at that time I had my ambulance uniform on – a collar and tie and also my hair was short – that's just because of being on twenty-four hour duty and ready to go out at a minute's notice. I think because of how I looked, she felt she could be attracted to me. But it was there anyway. I got out of the taxi dazed, because it was a long time since my last girlfriend – and then she said 'Will you meet me outside Whiteley's?' and I went to meet her again, and this went on for about a year, I think. Then I just got on to other relationships.

I didn't know many other lesbians then. I can remember being in the Underground and seeing someone who looked a bit 'butch' and thinking 'God! She's like me!' and being quite amazed and smiling over at this woman on the other platform. I can't remember what her reaction was. Well, you thought you were the only one because you didn't learn anything at school about it, and when my mother was with us she was getting us ready to be married, like all mothers, you know.

I know I went to the Gateways around 1944.[1] The Gateways must have been open then, because I remember clearly going down the King's Road round that period, and also I lived in Oakley Gardens, which is near the Club – off Oakley Street. The club was in Bramerton Street, down a flight of stairs. They had a trio there. It was usually women playing at that time. There was an old colonel who ran the Club, and it was very difficult to get in – I had to be taken in. You couldn't become a member, it was very exclusive in its way. They were arty types going down there, it wasn't really a lesbian club when he had it. Later, I think he sold the Club after I was around in Chelsea, living in that area. Then I found I could get in. That must have been the time when Ted Ware and his wife took over. So then everyone could get in. There was another club about that time, up in Tottenham Court Road, on the first floor. I think it was called the Jubilee. That was very good, a very nice club. I remember you could get spam and chips, very cheaply. And there was another club around the back streets of Tottenham Court Road, the Coffee Ann. It had wooden gates when you went in which you had to push, like a sort of stable or something, and there were pebbles on the ground. It was a very arty sort of place. People went in, but they weren't homosexual or lesbian necessarily – they were arty types mostly, or seemed to be.

When I went to the Gateways, the atmosphere was fantastic. For a start, we had women from overseas coming in, because they were stationed here, so you had all sorts of different people. Very interesting, very crowded, very packed. You got sightseers, of course, coming to look at all these people. People danced, especially during that war period when they were extra-enjoying themselves.

I was conscripted into the WAAF when I was twenty one. I remember that it was my birthday, and I remember my girlfriend seeing me off. I was driving – any vehicle – driving old colonels around. We also did square bashing and went on marches to raise money. Then I had a girlfriend in London, and I happened to hear that people were getting out of the WAAFs by being lesbians. So I thought that I would. I wanted to go back to London; I missed my lover. So I went to a psychiatrist, and I got out very easily. He just asked about how I felt when I saw a woman, about my reaction, I told him, and I was out very quickly. I went back to my girlfriend who was twenty years older than me. After that I still had to earn some money, so I went to the War Department again, and I worked there till the end of the war, as a driver.

I never really met any women except in the clubs – particularly the Gateways – and when I was on my own I went to the Gateways most evenings. There was role-playing and that was the way it was. If you weren't one way or the other, if you didn't conform, they derided you for it and said you didn't know what you were. If you were both ways, I think there was a name for it. In a way I suppose you take a stance anyway. It depends on your taste in partners. I liked particularly feminine women myself – a lot of women don't like the idea of that because they don't want a woman to be particularly feminine. So I always took the active role. I remember there was one very butch-looking woman there who had a terrible reputation because she used to get into bed with women and not do anything, and we all used to think it was terribly funny, which we shouldn't have really. But your reputation got around – what you were like, what you weren't like, and you were petrified of losing your reputation if it was a good one.

I felt happy in my butch role and not at all constrained by it. But when I was about twenty-six or twenty-seven, I remember I met a feminine, attractive woman and when we went to bed I didn't really feel attracted to her at that moment. Then I was shocked to find that she was making love to me. And I didn't mind, I rather liked it and it turned out very well with two active people making love. But I was petrified and told her not to tell anyone, which shows the atmosphere of the time. It's difficult when you've been doing things one way for a long time, and people in the club are saying you should be this or that – and being petrified that it was going to get around. But, in fact, I discovered that it was much better for both to be active, you know.

I was very happy being lesbian. I didn't wish to have any other way of living so I had no hang-ups about it. I've always loved being with women. I didn't feel I was anything extraordinary, so I've always lived my life the way it was. But I've had several nasty remarks now and again. I remember walking up the King's Road once and a man said, 'God, if you knew what you looked like, you wouldn't dress like that.' All I had on was trousers from my uniform and a jacket. I just thought 'Silly old sod.' No one could get me down at that age – I was full of myself and I took no notice. But I've had several incidents like that. Once two blokes came along behind us and said 'Get off the pavement you fucking lesbians.' And I said 'I'm not going to get off the pavement, I'll knock your fucking teeth in.' They replied, 'At least you've got some guts, so you can go then.' But I remember that very well indeed. Some things you just can't erase from your memory: the hate that came out that night.

All my working life I had to listen to women talking about their children and the washing and their husbands which I considered very frustrating, as I couldn't, or didn't, say 'I'm a lesbian' because they wouldn't have understood, and I didn't want to lose their friendship. I don't think heterosexuals will ever understand. They might tolerate us, but that's about all I think you can hope for.

One of my brothers saw me in a club years ago, and I was dancing and being very affectionate with a woman. I glanced across and saw him and we both had a terrible shock. After that, he was very odd towards me. My other brother thinks I hate men. This is because I tried to talk to my mother about feminism. I don't hate men, I just don't see them. But I tried to talk to her about how some men hate women.

I'm half Italian. I remember going to the cinema with my grandmother who didn't speak any English. There was a boy behind who tapped me on the shoulder. He asked 'Are you one of the Ginelli family?' I said, 'Yes', and he said 'Did you know that your grandfather used to chase half the little boys in Viareggio?' I said, 'No, I didn't.' Evidently, he was quite notorious. Another aunt of mine who I visited in Viareggio had a young girl, about sixteen. Very attractive little thing. She always ate with us, and Maria – this aunt of mine – always made such a fuss of this young girl. I didn't realise until later that she must have had a thing about this young girl. She never had anything to do with men, so I realised she also was probably lesbian. Of course, to be homosexual is frowned upon more in Italy than it is in a lot of countries.

I'm fairly happy with my life – I wish I'd done more – as a matter of fact I met someone several months ago, and I had hopes that it was going to blossom – she's seventy-seven, and I fell for her like a ton of bricks. I only wish it had happened to me when I was younger. I couldn't believe it, that I was so attracted by her. We'd only met three times. I sent poetry to her like mad. Alas, this turned out to be a holiday romance. My love for women has never diminished. They still make my blood tingle or my heart ache.

NOTES

1. See Note 1 after the introduction.

SYLVIA

I was born in 1921, and my younger brother and I had a normal childhood. Sex was not discussed in those days, but from the age of eleven I started to fall in love with girls. But when it became rather emotional my mother tended to ridicule my feelings. When she began to ridicule them, I kept them secret. I never talked about my feelings. Deep down I must have known they were unacceptable. I never dated boys, and I always knew I would never marry.

At twenty, as a university student, I started attending a High Anglican church. All my sexual energy was then channelled into my religion, although I was quite unaware of what was happening. There was no one with whom I could discuss all this. I became very depressed. I think it was because I wasn't fitting in. Everybody else was getting engaged and married and I didn't seem to have a plan at all. So I became rather depressed, and I went to my doctor who sent me to a psychiatrist twice a week for a year, and then once a week for the next year. I think he could have helped me, but you see he was trying to make me heterosexual. Looking back on it now, I'm quite surprised. Perhaps he wouldn't have done so now, but this was over thirty years ago. I remember he said one day 'You're more heterosexual than you used to be.' But I wasn't. Soon I began to think I had a vocation to the religious life. By this time, I had graduated and was teaching. I was a frequent visitor at an Anglican Convent, where the Reverend Mother and Novice Mistress made much of me. I decided to try my vocation there. My first weeks as a postulant were blissful. I thought it was for spiritual reasons, but I now realise that I was deeply in love with the Novice Mistress. The love became obsessive and I had erotic fantasies about her, which caused me to feel guilty. The tension mounted and my nerve began to crack. At last I knew I should leave, but I could not explain why. Afterwards I wrote and told them why I'd left and, later, when my mother died, I wrote and asked them if I could go back, but they wouldn't have me.

It was after I left the convent, in my next teaching job, that I fell in love with a member of staff and she fell in love with me. She was more experienced than I was, and she knew how to arouse me. Then I saw the danger signal and I was absolutely terrified. She wanted to get me into bed and I refused. I was terrified of the idea. I thought she might do something to harm me, either physically or psychologically. I was so ignorant, you see. It was quite agonising really, because I felt so guilty about the whole thing. Now, looking back on it, I think it was all very innocent, but in the end I couldn't endure it any longer. So I found myself another job quite a long way away from her. That caused me a lot of anguish, of course. So I ran away you see. I've been running away from such relationships ever since.

I did another very drastic thing. I left the Church of England and went into the Roman Catholic Church. It was an attempt to start again, I think. I had this idea that I'd done something impure and that I had betrayed Christ. So I went for instruction in the Roman Catholic Church where I was teaching, and, when I was received, I had to make a general confession. The priest was very good and asked me a lot of questions so that he would be sure to cover everything in my life. 'Well,' he said, 'have you ever done any impure things?' and I said, 'Yes.' And he said, 'By yourself or with others?' And I said, 'Both.' And then he said, 'With girls or boys?' And I said, 'Girls.' And then he went on to the next thing. That was all, you see. And I felt that cleansed me; I'd finished then. I must leave it and not have any relationships like that. In fact, looking back on it now, I don't think anything I did was impure. I think the whole episode was unnecessary. I came out of the Roman Catholic Church after five years. I couldn't stand it any longer. It had its advantages, but I didn't agree with so much that it taught. So I came back to the Church of England. But they're not very sympathetic in the C of E. I still go to confession in the C of E but the clergy are not sympathetic to homo-erotic people. They're not helpful. Just occasionally I've found one who is. My friends are very prejudiced against homosexuality, so I cannot be honest with them. All the other people I've loved – I have loved a lot of women – have been so high-principled that everything had to be expressed in non-sexual ways.

The word 'lesbian' was never used among my friends and family. I still don't like it very much. I prefer to be called homo-erotic because, after all, what does lesbian mean? It means a female homosexual and I've had no sex, so it's better to call me homo-erotic. I have to be very secretive about this because my brother and his wife would reject me, I think. At least they would be horrified, although I'm absolutely celibate, always have been. I'm sure they would disapprove and be quite appalled. I think that's the hardest thing – not being able to talk about it. Not being able to tell anyone, to have to keep everything secret, because I'm a very honest person. I like to talk about things and about my emotions. But I can't do it. I can't tell any of my friends, they're all terribly prejudiced. They think it's a perversion, you see.

I found a priest who understood me, an Anglican priest, and he advised me not to be so negative about it. This priest said it was not too late. But sometimes I feel that it is. You have to find the right person. He did try to find me a person, at the church, and I tried very hard, but she would have been horrified. It was quite impossible to arrive at any kind of intimacy. I like her very much, but I think she finds me absolutely outrageous. She thinks I'm a radical feminist.

She's very beautiful, two years younger than I. I feel I've known her all my life. She's not married. I think she would have been ideal, but I think I must have done something to frighten her away, although I was very delicate indeed. I didn't 'shoot my traces' or anything like that, but . . . something frightened her away, obviously. I can never see her without her sister now.

Of course, I have paid the price for all this in nervous tension: insomnia, eczema. I am also conditioned to feel guilty about loving other women, and I am probably quite incapable of expressing love in any physical way. I think it's rather late for me to establish a fulfilling relationship now. You have to meet the right person and it becomes less easy to travel about and meet people as you get older. Perhaps I shall be given another incarnation. I should like another incarnation, in which I could declare myself for what I am – find my soul-mate and have a kind of fulfillment that I haven't been able to have. That would be very nice.

I think it's the climate of opinion that has made us think it is a sin. Everything is geared and oriented towards the family and all kinds of horrific things happen in families. It's by no means the healthy relationship it's made out to be.

I now support Kenric[1] and the Gay Christian Movement, because it is the only way I can help other people to avoid the deprivation that I have borne all my life. We must change people's attitude if we are to stop unnecessary suffering, but how can we do that when we are all condemned to silence?

NOTES

1. *In 1965 two women from the Kensington and Richmond regional group of* Arena 3 *set up* Kenric *as a social group for lesbians. It continues to exist, produces a newsletter, has many social events and a network throughout the country. Contact Kenric, BM Kenric, London WC1V 6XX.*

PAT G.

I was born in the baby boom years after the First World War, in 1920. There were just little boys where I grew up. I didn't see anything amiss in that. I took it as normal – my poor mother used to get me up in nice dresses, silk socks and all that kind of thing and I'd be down at the garage in the motor oil in no time at all.

We moved to Brighton in 1928 – and I've hated Brighton from that day to this. Nothing nice ever happened to me in Brighton. We knew great poverty, we nearly had to go into the workhouse, but we children would have gone into something called Warren Farm, separate from our parents, but it didn't quite happen. There was a public canteen, a soup kitchen, and we sat there with tramps and I remember the smell of the boiled rice to this day.

I left school at fourteen – jobs were very difficult to get . It was Christmas 1934. I did get a job though, within ten days. It was pretty ghastly, it was in a laundry-receiving office. I had a box on wheels – I could hardly see over the top of it and I had to push this up and down the hills, picking up the daily washing, taking it to this office and sorting it – then going back the rest of the week with the clean. I used to pick up one shilling a week in tips – imagine! And I got ten shillings a week, which I'd hand over to my dad and he'd give me back one shilling, and that was tremendous riches. Eventually, I bought my first bike – a lovely green one. It was £3–19–9d, and I had it on hire purchase, two bob a week. That lasted until I was in the army – I used to keep it in my bedroom, go out with it before breakfast every morning.

Then I got a job in an engineering firm on the Lewes Road. It was there I met this woman – obviously she was a lesbian. Of course, I didn't realise it then. She was about twelve years older than me. I joined the ATS in 1938 and the following year we went on a summer camp with the Royal Sussex Regiment for a week. That was absolutely marvellous, I really enjoyed that. I came back full of it and it was then she made her little speech. She said, 'Somebody she knew', but, of course, she was talking about herself, and I was absolutely amazed. I'd never even suspected anything like that. She said, 'Oh, one day you're going to fall in love with another girl' and I just looked at her as if she was crazy. I'd always had these very idealised thoughts about friendship – it was very important to me especially friendship between girls – my contemporaries. We had to think things out for ourselves. I mean, there was no media – we didn't have a radio at home and if we had there wouldn't have been anything of 'that sort' to listen to and I didn't read newspapers in those days. Anyhow, within a matter of weeks of that summer camp I was called up and, of course, was in a terrible state of mind by then. It was also in 1938 that I'd become a Catholic. Although nothing of 'that sort' had ever been mentioned – I didn't know why I was suddenly so guilty about it. Guilt is such a peculiar thing: why be guilty when no one's ever said a thing is wrong? But somehow some conditioning said 'This isn't on.' I'd be walking home with this girl or that girl and sometimes we'd go on the beach with some chips. I'd be so thrilled to be with them and again, I didn't know how to cope with these emotions. I really didn't know what was happening to me. Then we were called up, so I was terrified in case I 'did' something – goodness knows what I thought I might do – I was just terrified at the thought I might.

The odd girl would make a pass at you – go to grab you – I took no notice of that . . . I was constantly being attracted by women, I would have been awfully active if I'd allowed myself to be in my twenties. I'd never heard the word 'lesbian' and when I finally did hear it I couldn't say it for years. It seemed such an ugly word – I didn't mind the word 'homo', somehow that was more acceptable. Very strange.

All my life, wherever I've looked, I have felt I was the only one. You would think that on the law of averages, whatever organisation you joined there would be more lesbians than just yourself at any given time. But it seems to me for the most part, unless I'm in something that I absolutely know is a gay organisation – I either can't recognise them in another situation – or they really aren't there. I don't know. You see, you'd expect to find a lot in the army – by the nature of things, but I didn't. So I had no experience at all in the army.

In 1944 I was ill and in and out of hospital, and I felt on the scrap heap. I saw this photo of girls on the canals and I really wanted to do that and rehabilitate myself. I was lucky enough to be taken on. All sorts of people were there – Susan Wolfitt, Donald's first wife; Jean Wells, niece of HG Wells; it was marvellous. You'd fill up with the stuff at Regent's Dock, travel through the 145 locks to Birmingham, unload, over to Coventry, fill up with coal and then go back. A three-week round trip, it was absolutely marvellous. I was never healthier in my life – out in all weathers, all day, every day. There were three in the crew, and Kay and Susan used to wander around in birthday suits, but that didn't disturb me because I was very smitten with Kay – she was the first person who ever kissed me and I was absolutely breathless. That was at Leicester.

The war ended and we came off the boats. Kay had a flat in Notting Hill and she sub-let it to me. It was quite a riotous time and we were drinking a lot. She said to me one day, 'I think I must be a lesbian.' I laughed and said 'Oh, no, not you' – as if I was saving her from something really quite ghastly. That was really an open invitation. I was so stupid. I took rather a long time to grow up.

Then I started on my second ambition and, in 1947, I became a student nurse, which fulfilled all my ambitions for caring. I went on having these pashes. But I was getting no encouragement, nobody fell for me you see, I was doing all the pursuing. Then I went back to Catholicism and a particular friend of mine, whom I fancied, was going to enter a convent, so I decided I would do that too. But just after I'd qualified as a nurse, and shortly before I was due to enter the convent, I spent the evening with a student nurse whom I went about with. We were in her room and she began tickling me and I said, 'Don't do that!' but she persisted. So I spent quite a bit of that night with her – again, not properly undressed. I crept out at dawn back to my place. I felt absolutely physically sick the next morning, and I'd actually got bite marks on my neck. I was so overwhelmed. There was I, committed to going into the convent and this had happened. I felt Hell's Gates practically opening up. So I went to the convent and told the sister who sent me to the priest. Actually nothing had happened. He knew more than I what could have happened. I mean, it was years and years before I did know. Curiously enough, a patient told me when I was district-nursing. Anyway, I went off to the covent, and, of course, I felt desperately lonely because I missed the warmth of friendship so much – it was called 'particular friendships' if you took notice of anybody. It became a greater and greater strain but I did stick to it for six years. I was meant to come home in 1956. I was given an extension, but I left before the end of it. Shortly after, I realised my mother was entering her final illness – cancer. I nursed my mother. She lasted eighteen months. I was district-nursing by then. Then I had five years on my own, which were ones of great loneliness and desolation.

Then I got myself out of district-nursing into a small country hospital. And there was this tiny little thing, Jill. I was absolutely smitten. She was really the love of my life. To me, she was somebody who desperately needed love and I felt I could make up for her hard background. I could give her a home. She came thinking she was going to be my lodger. She hadn't got any other ideas. She was very fond of me, I think, but never anything 'like that'. So I had another six years of loneliness. I was absolutely burned up about her, but never able to do anything about it.

So, in 1969, I finally decided it was time to grow up. And I thought, 'Now, you've really got to find out: are you or aren't you? You've really got to face this out. You've wasted enough years for goodness sakes.' So my remedy . . . I don't know why I thought of that really . . . I knew about the 'Gates'[1] and I thought I must go and get a look at them, see what I feel – like going to the zoo! I think they'd advertised in *Arena 3*,[2] for which I'd found an ad in the back of the *Nursing Mirror*. But in those days, one was even scared to send off for something within plain cover, which is so ridiculous, but that's how one was.

And finally, on my own, I dared to go there. Yes, I must have heard of it through that. And I joined Kenric.[3] You could go in on a Monday evening as a Kenric member – you didn't have to belong to the 'Gates'. So, there was I on this Monday, I'd travelled up from Horsham, I was doing a day's shopping. I was in my little newly made *Daily Telegraph* tweed dress. I left all my shopping at the station and I walked up and down the King's Road – absolute butterflies, and it was still only early evening. Finally I summed up courage to knock on the grilled door. There were very few people there at that hour, but even those that there were – well, my eyes nearly popped out – they were the extremes of both kinds. And then gradually, as the evening went on, the strangeness wore off, of course, and I realised I fitted in. I was the same: there was my answer! So I realised I must do something about it then. I simply felt comfortable, as I never had done with people ever before. I was in a situation so different – it's not tangible, you can't describe it. But it was there. It was a reality, it was enough. I didn't need convincing.

The people I would really like to meet – they just haven't fallen my

73

way. And that's it, that's the luck of the draw, so to speak. But I'm perfectly sure that there are a lot more people out there like me. I just haven't happened to meet them. I don't think I'm odd or peculiar – I mustn't say that these others are – but we just don't see things in the same way. That's the way it is. But I understand so much more now, and I'm at peace with myself.

NOTES

1. See Note 1 *after the introduction.*
2. See Note 3 *after the introduction.*
3. See Note 1 *after Sylvia's story.*

SHARLEY MCLEAN

Going back to my childhood – I had a very good friend, – you know your 'best friend' and, when she was about thirteen or fourteen she started having boyfriends and I could never understand why on earth she should prefer a boyfriend to me – so it was there, latent – I just didn't understand it at all.

I came to England as a refugee from Germany, so I was a German in Britain during the War. A friend of mine was an orderly in Lewisham Hospital and she used to say to me 'You're one of us' – and I used to feel so flattered because I thought she meant I came over as 'British', you know, 'one of us', but of course she didn't mean that at all, you see – but it took me quite a few years to find out what the hell she did mean!

I was horribly ignorant really. I realised I wasn't very turned on by men, but I did marry – there were all sorts of pressures, sort of running away from things – I don't know, it's very hard to be positive. I do know I found anything sexual rather disgusting. When I became pregnant with my second child, I thought, 'Well, this is it.' It was an excuse for no further sexual activities. After the child was born, I kept on thinking up more excuses and there came a time when I couldn't think up any more and I just went into hysterics. I felt I could no longer cope living like that, and I tried to commit suicide.

75

This was in 1950 and suicide was still an indictable offence then, and it was decided that I would not be charged with anything if I should seek psychiatric help. I saw a psychologist – probably she was a lesbian – but she told me that's what I was. I didn't believe her. I mean, there were all the negative feelings and all the negative things one had heard about this sort of thing, and I really didn't believe her. I remember when I came out of this session at the Tavistock Clinic, I walked to Marble Arch and somehow found myself in Selfridges. I had just drawn my family allowance, and I was quite well off economically, I went to the coat department and bought a coat, the most hideous coat you could wish to buy – and I never wore it. I never wore it. You know this was the sort of reaction one had. The shock. I was thinking about what she had said and I can imagine it's something like when people tell me now that they have been diagnosed anti-body positive. You think only of the negative, you think of death, you wouldn't think of life – and that's probably how I was. What an awful situation to live with and wondering how I would cope. Fortunately, I had further sessions at the Clinic which obviously helped. And then working through things, I soon realised she was right.

I remember going to the Gateways[1] after that. I knocked on the door and walked in, and I thought 'Oh, God, this isn't me!' I felt totally out of place, and I think I stayed five minutes before disappearing. I should not have gone alone. I should have given myself more time, but I was curious. I wanted to meet my tribe, so to speak, I suppose.

I was twenty-seven then and my notion of a lesbian which was a little bit reinforced when I went to the Gateways Club, was of women in tweeds and very, very loud, and butch, wearing these pseudo-male hats, and cracking the whip, so to speak. I later realised that they were not all like that but just ordinary women. Well, I mean I was ordinary too.

I subsequently met a young woman at a club I used to frequent, and

76

we had an affair for quite a short time, but it was enough to sort of make me realise yes, this was the right thing for me. I mean, I shall never forget it. It's hard to convey the complex feelings I have about how precious time with other lesbians was and the miserable, every day repression we returned to. I had to build up an alibi at home – I had two small children and you can't just walk out on two small children. It was summer – my lover had this grotty bedsitter – right under the roof and you could hear the mice scuttling about and I'm afraid of mice – but I completely forgot about them. So that was really marvellous. It was my very first lesbian experience, and I've never forgotten it.

I don't quite know how I viewed homosexuality. I had an uncle in Germany who I knew was homosexual, and he was actually one of those people with a pink triangle. He was very much loved, and there wasn't any talk about there being anything wrong with him. I know I had an aunt who never married and had very close women friends, but she would never have labelled herself a lesbian. And I also had a cousin in exactly the same situation. I've also heard I have a niece, but does it run in families? I really don't know.

It took me years to come out, but I had definitely come out by the time my daughter was seven in 1953. I started a relationship with Georgina very soon after that which lasted for twenty-four years. I never got a divorce. I went to see a lawyer, and he said it would make front page news, and it was better not to get a divorce. But if my husband wanted it, let him divorce me – which seemed pretty good advice. So it made it easier for the children, and we still share a house. He was never around, and we've lived separately all these years.

My daughter, Jeannie, had always been asked at school 'What is your religion?' and I obviously used to say, 'Oh, we haven't got any,' or 'We're humanists' or 'atheists' or 'agnostics', or whatever, and she couldn't make this out. I think my sister-in-law realised I was a lesbian then – although I wasn't in an affair or anything – but she had obviously screamed down something at me like 'You're a lesbian' and

Jeannie had picked this up. She was young then, she was still in the infants'. And she asked me 'What does it mean to be a lesbian?' I felt at that age it was much too young to say anything, and I must have said, 'Well, it's my religion.' Anyway, she went back to school and told the teacher, 'Now I know what we are, we're lesbians.' The reason I know that, is because at an open day the teacher collared me and I didn't know where to put myself.

A few years later, I told my daughter and she understood. It was easier to explain then. My son used to bring friends home who he thought might be gay, and I could talk to their parents. That often worked. I was also having a relationship with Georgina and my children knew about her. She was like a second mum to them and they loved her and they understood.

I was always interested in women and politics. I campaigned very early on in women's rights. We did not meet all that many lesbians, or people we were aware of being lesbians. Later on we realised they were. People did not really come out – you sort of got a feeling about a person, but that's all. It wasn't really until towards the end of the sixties that one felt much more comfortable. Georgina, unfortunately, remained very closeted, and I had to respect her feelings. After all, it was our relationship that was of paramount importance. Campaigning around lesbian issues didn't seem important then – it was campaigning around women's issues. I think to have come out as lesbian in those days would have been totally impossible. I think you were aware of a pressure, you didn't really test it.

One year Georgina was going to spend Christmas with her family. Her whole family was going to be there. She left London on 23 December, promising to 'phone me. Our arrangement had always been that I would not 'phone her when she visited her family, since she was closeted, and I went along with that. Her illusion was that after twenty-four years being together her family would still be unaware of our lifestyle.

There was no 'phone call, not even at Christmas. When I could endure the silence no longer, I decided to 'phone. Someone answered and I asked to speak to Georgina, the reply was: 'She's dead', and down went the receiver. I rang again and again – different voices replied, hostile, nasty, abusive, refusing to give me any real information. Eventually a woman who identified herself as the niece was especially venomous, that special brand of abuse, calculated cruelty and that power to inflict hurt. She told me that Georgina had had a heart attack, then gleefully that I was to blame. Photos had been found and destroyed, she ended up by giving me totally wrong information regarding the funeral arrangements and saying 'We don't want you there . . . you have nothing to do with her!'

I was too numb to do very much, walking around like a zombie totally unable to believe what I had heard. I took good old tranquillisers; my daughter was of immense support; colleagues at work considered, well . . . just a friend . . . that's how they wanted to see it.

I went to the flat, I had waited too long, everything had been stripped, no trace of our things . . . everything cleared out . . . as though we had never been there. I think it was then that I finally accepted that Georgina was dead.

I find it near impossible to attend funerals, the few that I went to left me devastated for weeks, as I was unable to go to hers. I also display a violent anger against parents and relations who deny the dead or dying children their sexuality. The loss of a loved person causes an ache which is breath-catching, my memory of Georgina is her reincarnation . . . she lives on.

After Georgina died I threw myself into gay politics, and from the point of view of grieving, it helped me tremendously to come to terms with her death. My daughter was very supportive, but all the other people around couldn't understand it.

It was quite a horrendous time. Looking back, I suppose we lived half a life. It's easier now, it's better now. There are meeting-places, which is marvellous, we didn't have that. We had to move in a heterosexual world. Often, from that point of view, we were feeling isolated because we couldn't talk about what we felt. The realisation of how one had missed out, I think that hit you eventually. I became pretty active in lesbian and gay politics. I still campaign around Hyde Park Gays and Sapphics every Sunday. I feel that at least that's using something to make people aware. With Section 28,[2] you can really get your teeth into something again.

People get to recognise you, and I was waiting outside the committee offices, and this guy drove past, he put his head out the window, shouting, 'You're a lesbian!' 'Yes, I know,' I replied. He was totally deflated. I don't care. I've only ever been threatened once seriously. I've been harassed on the underground, and a couple of punks came to protect me. We've been threatened in the park and pushed off the platform at Speakers' Corner. We try and never stay alone in any situation like that. We've only had one policeman who's been really nasty. Usually when I call for help, I've been given it.

I think Section 28 is horrendous. It brings out all my old fears. I'm neurotic about it, because this is how it started in Germany – not with a Section 28, but with the implications of it. I'm frightened because it's not the first thing that's happened here – trade unions are being torn to shreds, the press, the way they report trade union activity . . . you can see the facts are never really presented. Lies are being told – the workforce is already split. And this is how it started in Germany. The racism – although there are laws against it, one is aware of it. Such as the anti-semitism that is fostered, about what is happening in Israel. I've never been pro an Israeli state because I'm an anarchist, and I'm fully aware that when you have a state, no matter what, any power is evil. I know they said Section 28 was only really going to affect schools – talking about homosexuality in schools – but the implications are so wide. It really is frightening, it scares me to death. When I hear people argue glibly about it, and when I hear gay people and lesbians say to me, 'Why do you campaign about it? Why must you stand up and shout about it? It's people like you who've brought it about' I think to myself, 'Where have they lived?' And this is what frightens me. I think I can't possibly live through another form of discrimination like that. They want to drive us back into the closet and make us liars again. That really gets right under my skin – not to be able to say 'Well, I'm a lesbian. I'm a gay man. That's how I am and that's right for me. You're happy as heterosexual.' I think the OLGA card 'It takes two heterosexuals to make one homosexual' is lovely. I sent one of those to my MP.

In the past, we were hidden. We weren't allowed to be truthful about ourselves. We were much too frightened. And I think that was the worst thing, in a way. You had to lie about yourself. I am aware that I resented that. I resented it very, very much, having to pretend to be something you weren't. But when I came out at work, I know I helped a lot of other lesbians there who came out – to me, at least. So in a way you were doing something positive for other women, and that was important. So it makes you realise you're not on your own – there are loads of us.

NOTES

1. *See Note 1 after the introduction.*
2. *See Note 2 after the introduction.*

RUTH MAGNANI

Oh, I can remember very well when I first thought I might be a lesbian. It was in September, 1970. I had been married for over twenty years. My mother was a French woman who was very conventional, and she thought that if you hadn't caught a man and got married – well, you just didn't exist. I won't dwell too much on my marriage, but he was an alcoholic, treated me and my children very badly. I think that says everything, doesn't it? He was very violent, and when they say there is no rape within marriage, I could actually disprove that. I had very bad experiences at my husband's hands, but I have to admit that because I had children growing up, I didn't consciously seek a way out. I had three children – one of whom is autistic.

I have always had a job – I've had to deal with the sort of man who doesn't provide for his family which means that it's up to the woman to do something about it. I went out to work, and I graduated from jobs to careers. One of the things I did – while I was still technically living with my husband – I ran an arts festival in the village where I was living – I used to be in the theatre, years and years ago. And the person who did my publicity was a gay woman. It didn't occur to me that there was anything there other than friendship, and she was very supportive.

83

Well, after a bit I became very reliant on her. I found I just couldn't envisage life without her suppport and friendship. She had a partner, and made no bones about it, and I really believed that she just saw me in the light of a friend who was going through a bad time. But I also realised that I was becoming very, very attracted to her. Although there was no question of a permanent relationship there, we did have an affair. I knew it would never come to anything but it opened up a whole new world for me. I suddenly realised what it meant to have the love and support of a woman, and for the first time in my life, I felt attractive, wanted, needed and appreciated. And it just grew on from there.

Once I'd had that experience, I understood the things I'd felt when I was younger, the deep friendships I'd formed with other women. Suddenly, it all fell into place. Of course, we're going back a few years now, when lesbians didn't talk about being lesbians. It was just those two funny school teachers, you know, who lived down the end of the street, or "funny women" – 'Pity they never got married, such nice people, but they didn't get married – shame isn't it? Spinsters' – and all this sort of thing. I was conditioned into thinking that the married state was a very desirable one. But as I say, as soon as I'd had that experience, it all just fell into place.

Well, the relationship broke up, thanks to reasons that are many and complex. But having parted from this relationship, very reluctantly, I then sat down – I'm a very practical lady – and I made up my mind what I was going to do. I said 'Obviously, this is for me. That was where I was happy, that was where I was fulfilled. So I shall just set about finding someone of my own.' So I did.

I didn't have the nerve to just arrive at a gay club, but then I've never been good at going into pubs on my own. I was determined, nevertheless, that I was going to find someone. I found out about *Sappho*[1] magazine simply by asking questions, and ringing people up, and I put in an ad. But for eighteen months afterwards, I did nothing. I was simply very, very unhappy. Luckily I was mature enough to know that not anybody would do – it had to be the right person. So, perhaps in a way I was saved a lot more unhappiness.

I had twenty-eight replies to this ad – one woman who replied sounded nice – well, pleasant – and she was married and I thought, 'Well, I don't fancy a woman who is still married.' But then, you know, in the letter of the law, I was still married, so it could be all right. So we started a correspondence – she lived in Devon, and I was living outside Southampton. One Sunday morning, I had the radio on, and I was bopping around the kitchen, aiming the duster in a sort of desultory fashion, and the front door bell rang. When I opened it, there was this very small lady with dyed blond hair, and she said, 'Are you Ruth?' 'Yes.' 'Ooh, I'm Kate, we've been writing to each other.' I said, 'Oh, yes.' And she said 'I've brought my husband along.' And before you could say 'homosexual', she bounced in and so did he. He was an enormous bloke, and I thought, 'He's come to duff me up.' He sat down and said to me, 'Well, my dear, my wife has explained to me her needs. I do realise that her needs are not the same as my needs. But I would like to see that she gets what she wants, but I'm not sure how we're going to do it, you see, because we've got the children, and the youngest one is very young. And my wife, of course, she's very fond of children, and she wouldn't want to leave 'em. So I consider the best thing you can do is pack your bags and come home with us.' So I said, 'You're not serious, are you?' and he said, 'Well, why not? I'm not looking for anything at all. I understand. But there's only one stipulation I must make. Are you listening?' And I said, 'Yes, I'm listening with bated breath.' And he said, 'Well, you can sleep with her all week, but she has to sleep with me at the weekends. 'Tis only fair, innit?' And that, if I never move again, is what happened! After this I'd given up, because I thought if everyone was a nutcase like this, I would be much better off on my own.

Then this letter came, and I'll always remember it. It was twelve pages, written on both sides, and it was a very good letter – articulate – and the woman, Pat, told me all about herself, about her circumstances, and she said what she was looking for was a one-to-one relationship, a permanency. She wanted to settle down and she wanted someone to love and care for. And she wanted the person in her life to feel that way about her. I thought, 'Ah, now, this sounds like me.' Anyway, we started to exchange letters, and we wrote for about a month. Then we arranged to meet. She arrived at half past seven in the morning, having driven about four hours from her home. She came to the door, and I thought, 'According to how she is, you either shake hands with her or you give her a peck on the cheek. Be very calm, cool and collected.' So I opened the door, she came in, and I thought, 'This is definitely a kiss on the cheek type.' So I reached up and kissed her on the cheek and said, 'Welcome.' She put her arms around me and that was that. I think it took ten minutes for us to come out of the hall. I got her breakfast for her, and she ate it all, and said it felt as if she'd sat there all her life. It was marvellous, absolutely marvellous. The weekend was an absolute daze of happiness. I just can't tell you. I often go over it again and again in my mind, because nothing is so perfect as that first time when it hits you, wham, between the eyes. We've lived together ever since, and this year we'll have lived together for seventeen years.

Pat introduced me to *Kenric*[2] because it had a lot of social things going on, and I'm a very social person – I love people and I love parties. I like getting out and about and enjoying myself. The biggest plus for me is that gay people within their own circle never seem to grow old. Now I like dancing and if I went to a heterosexual disco, everyone would say 'What's that silly old bag doing here? What does she think she's doing?' But as it is, I can go to a gay disco and dance the night away. No one thinks it's strange. You know, I'm sorry for people who aren't gay – they miss so much. I don't mean I'm the oldest swinger in town and I *must* go to a disco, but it's lovely to feel that if you're at a social gathering and somebody puts on a record, or a tape, or a group starts up, that you can get up and nobody says, 'Oh, poor old soul, what does she think she's doing?' And I have a whale of a time because I just love it. I love music, I love dancing, I love people. It's a big bonus, it's great! God, if I hadn't discovered what I have discovered, I'd probably be sitting here knitting for my grandchildren. I've never regretted it for a moment.

My daughters didn't speak to me for about three years. My first reaction was one of immense regret because I didn't want to alienate my daughters but I was also quite unprepared to give up the happiness I'd found. I'd always been the sort of mother that had allowed her children to make their own decisions. Sometimes disastrously, but I figured it was their life and I was a bit shattered to find out that the same rules didn't apply to me. It was very sad, very sad indeed. They didn't like Pat, they loathed her. There were a lot of faults on both sides. I think Pat was quite jealous of the way I felt about them, and they were certainly very jealous, because she'd taken over my life, as they saw it. They were both in their teens, and I said to them 'Look, my dears, you've always demanded the right to do your own thing, so, by the same token, that is my right as well.' And although they didn't like it, they had to accept it.

They felt I had been lured. They felt that if only they could get me out of this woman's clutches, it would be all right. The funny thing was that the person who gave me the hardest time was probably my youngest daughter, who had had a great deal to do with gay people. Some of the gay men she knew she had introduced me to, and she'd grown up with friends of mine who were gay. She'd spent lots and lots of time with them. But it's acceptable in other people – it's not acceptable in your mother. Mother must be like Caesar's wife, she must be above reproach. It's just never occurred to me that people don't have the right to live their own lives. I've never felt guilty or ashamed or closeted or anything like that. I just totally accept that it's happened to me, and it's given me so much happiness – how can it be wrong?

I suppose I'm a bit like the Born Again Christians when they're first converted. I was so over the moon, and I was so happy, that when people asked about the relationship, I was totally open. And I didn't realise that this was something you didn't do too much. I did find a lot of discrimination. Men used to be very abusive, very nasty. We had a man who lived three doors away, and he taught his children to call after us. The children didn't even know what they were calling. Another time a little girl ran up to me and said, 'Look, Auntie Ruth, look what I've got!' and her mother said, 'Come away, don't you dare speak to that woman! She's dirty – come away.' And I could see this child looking so bewildered, you know, looking at me as if to say 'Well, where are you dirty? Where's the dirt?' I've had a lot of discrimination at work, particularly in the advertising business, but never from the creative side. It was the accountants, the administrative staff – secretaries loathed me. It's very hurtful when you go in every day and you get cold-shouldered. Yes, I suffered a great deal of discrimination – at work, and ultimately I lost two jobs through being a lesbian. I just didn't realise that I would bring this storm down upon my head. And I then went to a situation where I did become, for quite a long time, closeted. I would not talk about it – and I was almost sorry that I had come out.

It changed mainly, I think, because I went to work in London for financial reasons. I met a lot of women there who were 'out'. And mixing with them, talking to them, I realised that I had nothing to lose at all, and that I should actually be spreading the gospel, and not just sitting behind my little professional desk at work, or anything like that.

I think we have a long way to go, but it's one of the reasons I agreed to appear in this programme. I feel that unless people are going to be very positive about what they're doing, then we haven't got a hope in hell of making the so-called straight world understand what we're all about. And we're about a lot of things. We're not only about having lesbian lovers, having sex, living with another woman – important though that all is. We're about the whole situation of women, in what is still very much a male-dominated society. And unless people

Rachel as she is now and as
she was in her school
uniform.

Left: Pat G. during the Second World War.

Bottom: Marie, Rosanna, Diana and Ceri.

Betty on holiday as a child and on her wedding day in 1954.

Left: Vick at home in Newcastle with her cat, Blossom.

Bottom: Ruth in her cottage in Cornwall.

Left: Nina as a child in Jersey.

Bottom: from left to right:
Betty, Nina, Rachel, Sally,
Ruth and Ellen on location in
Brighton.

Right: One of Ellen's first
girlfriends "Billy" around
1938.

Bottom: Ellen (*right*) and Ruth
relax during filming.

Publicity photo of Jackie in 1956/7 during her television career (*top*), and Jackie as she is now (*bottom*).

Right: Sally as a teenager with her friend.

Bottom: Dorothy dancing with Jackie at "The Only Alternative Left" in Hove during the filming of *Women Like That*.

like me – and let's face it, if you looked at me in the street, you wouldn't say 'Ah! That is a lesbian.' Would you? Unless people like me – very ordinary, normal, older women get up on their hind legs, and talk about themselves, and let the world know that we're not people with two heads, that we're not perverted, ghastly creatures who are going to do frightful things – Until that happens, then women are always going to be stuck away, in bad situations, in marriages, and in closets, and all the other things that are so detrimental to women as human beings.

I believe that on the surface, things have changed, quite a lot. There's a lot going on in the media about us, and people discuss it more. But it's very different when it's near home. On your doorstep! I still think parents are very shattered if they find out their children are gay or lesbian.

I would like to see a greater tolerance all round. Not just about gay sexuality, but a lot of other issues of discrimination too. I'd also like to see more openness about taboo subjects, such as physical and sexual abuse. People must open up more, talk to each other more, and learn to understand each other. But it needs to be something more than just understanding us, we have got to learn to live together and care about each other. And if we can get to that stage, I think that our situation will change quite a lot.

NOTES

1. *See Note 4 after Jackie Forster's story.*
2. *See Note 1 after Sylvia's story.*

JACKIE FORSTER

I went through all the heterosexual phase, and I didn't think about lesbianism until I had my first affair with a woman when I was 32 and married. I didn't consider myself a lesbian – just that I'd fallen in love for the first time, and was loved in a way I never, ever was with men. I was absolutely madly in love with this woman, and she with me, and I was completely taken over, physically and emotionally.

Oh, it was just euphoric madness, passion. I couldn't breathe and, you know, day in, day out having to have this kind of . . . juxtaposition where I'd never felt so alive, never felt so beautiful, never felt so part of the world – and all the colours and the lights! Yet at the same time it was this 'awful thing' which we mustn't talk about. So there was a great conflict going on. I couldn't really see why, especially when I felt so marvellous, and also the woman did too which I could see in her eyes, in the way we made love. So it was a real awakening *of* me. But at the same time, this hideous terror, you know, in case I am found out or in case somebody discovers us. And that's when I said 'Oh, I must be a lesbian.' And 'lesbian' in the fifties, as I understood it, was just a short back and sides woman, with a waistcoat and I never saw myself like that. And so I didn't identify as lesbian at all. When I first heard the word, I thought

'Ohhh, maybe this is what is happening to me.' And I'd sort of look in the mirror to see if I had a kind of leprosy coming, to see if this 'dreadful thing' was showing.

The only thing I'd ever read was *The Well Of Loneliness*. My lover was no Stephen Gordon,[1] and neither was I. And there was nowhere, nowhere at all we could go. It was the loneliness and the wondering where we fitted. Of course, we always dressed in dresses and matching accessories. So with *The Well Of Loneliness* in mind, and what I'd heard about lesbians – that they wore three-piece suits, short back and sides and cufflinks and things, I thought 'Why am I feeling so good?'

And with all this information in my head, I then had this tremendous explosion of an affair with no one to talk to, so I was in this real bind. I mean, I'm doing something 'evil', and I'll head for hell. I was this bad woman, and at the same time I was coming to life for the first time in my whole existence. Everything I'd been brought up to believe in made no sense at all. Where was my information? Where was my role model? You see, my lover was very much in the closet. She was a very grand lady.

She couldn't introduce me to her friends because they might suspect. And so, here again from her was this 'terrible thing', but inside I knew it was right but I couldn't talk about it. I didn't know who to talk to about it. So I had a lot of guilt and a lot of fear, but at the same time, this wonderful flood of passion and being in the world because she was there. When that affair ended, I went right back to the straight scene. I thought well I've known what love's like, I've been in love, and that's it. So I didn't go looking for other women. I didn't, in fact, know where to find them in the fifties. I didn't know where the bars were, that kind of thing. It wasn't until I was in Canada – some six years later and I met a woman then, and 'bammy', it happened all over again. That's when I thought, well now, this for me is the 'real thing' which happens with women in a way it's not been happening with men. In this second relationship, which lasted ten years, we both grew together, knowing that we didn't want any other woman to go through what we went through. This was in the sixties.

Then in 1964 *Arena 3* started up in London, and they had women only meetings. And we would go along there and help get out *Arena 3*[2] – which was the very first gay magazine – the term 'gay' was used then – published and run and written by lesbians. There was an amazing mix of women. They weren't like the stereotypical Gateways[3] of the early fifties. So I thought, and so did the people we were meeting, that we were sick and tired of being told what we were – from psychiatrists and others outside. We thought *no, we* know what we're about, we are the experts. And so we became rather political in *Arena 3*. We started talking about the whole dimension of women's sexuality. And we then said, 'Well, let's say "lesbian".' People said 'I don't like that word.' So we kept saying 'lesbian' and then claiming all the words – 'dyke' and 'diesel' and this kind of thing. I came out at Speakers' Corner in 1970, twelve years after my first affair, it took all that time. That really was my coming out. I felt I could say it to the world.

From *Arena 3*, which then – through in-fighting – closed, we moved into starting *Sappho*,[4] because women were saying we must keep in contact through a magazine. So we got *Sappho* together. And then, we were meeting women from everywhere, because we had subscribers from right around the world. And we had meetings every week and we had discos.

So there was a whole concept of women who loved women, were loved by women, who were as varied and different as any society or group of people anywhere. And we made ourselves very strong and proud. At the meetings and discos, I'd see women coming in like sort of stick insects, this terror of meeting your own kind, walking up and down outside before they'd come in. And I always made it a point just to take their elbow and say 'Welcome.' Their tension was unbelievable. And it's this terrible conflict women are having all the time about meeting openly and naturally as lesbians. It's still going on to this day.

I think I'm very lucky to have managed to move through into the situation as it is now, where there is so much choice, and there is a lesbian community. But why did I have to go through all that rubbish? I mean, it still hurts me, so when a woman's been in the closet and is talking now, I think 'You don't have to, you don't have to, it's in your head.' I'd remember myself there thinking 'What am I doing? What's going to happen to me?'

At one of the *Sappho* meetings, someone suggested a conference for married lesbians. Well I'd had an inhibition about married women coming along; were they wanting to see what it was like and just have a one-off? So I wasn't very pro married lesbians or lesbian mothers. But we set up a weekend where lesbian mothers could come and meet each other and talk about the problems, and announced it in *Sappho*. And to our astonishment, over a hundred women came, from as far as Cornwall and Devon and up North and Scotland. And it was an amazing revelation. They were all married, or they had left their husbands, and they all had children. It was an amazing weekend. All my prejudices went out of the window. So they started the Gay Wives and Mothers Group, which was mainly social. Childless lesbians, even if they were partners, weren't allowed, we had to take the kids off to the zoo. This was a wonderful breakthrough, and then, of course, some of them became very political. They became Action for Lesbian Parents and they went storming in to Elwyn-Jones, who was Labour Lord Chancellor, and said 'Look, all these custody cases going on are based on prejudice, and not justice.' He nearly had a fit. Now there are lots of lesbian mothers' groups – but in 1972 this was the first one. Then the Gay Teachers Group was formed out of a *Sappho* conference in 1974. Then the nurses wanted a conference, and we had 300 women and men there – and the Gay Medics Group was formed. And they all spun off into these national groups. There was an enormous sense of coming alive, they were such heady days, and we grew very political. The women's movement was coming into my life.

Meetings now are much more representative of the women who come and their concerns. And, really, I cannot believe in my lifetime it went from that darkness of the fifties to strolling into the London Lesbian and Gay Centre, or being on that marvellous Gay Pride march, where there were 30,000 of us.

When I went up to Manchester for the Clause 28[5] march, and saw those thousands of people there, it was what I always dreamed it would be. But there's still a hard core of society that needs changing. And I think we are in danger – that is all lesbians and gay men – because there can be really strong reactions to us, as with Clause 28. I think probably another part of society does that old thing of 'Well, it's none of my business what you do in bed', and you've got to keep saying, 'Yes, it *is*. Because of what I do in bed I lose my kids. Because of what I do in bed I lose my job. Because of what I do in bed I'm thrown out of the house or thrown out of the family,' But that hardcore of society is really influencing our laws and influencing education in schools – they see us as perverts who are corrupting society. And my view is we must never rest, we've got to go out there talking or reacting, very strongly. One thing I do think is that we must have become very powerful for Clause 28 to have been brought into the law.

Finally, I just hope that after women have got over the first nervous, tremulous crossing of the threshold, that they have the full passionate, wonderful, emotional experiences I've had, and can be utterly open with other women.

NOTES

1. *Stephen Gordon is the main female character in Radclyffe Hall's book* The Well of Loneliness. *Stephen is described as an 'invert' and dresses in male attire.*
2. *See Note 3 after the introduction.*
3. *See Note 1 after the introduction.*
4. Sappho *magazine was formed after the collapse of* Arena 3 *in 1971. Women continued to meet in the Museum Tavern, Museum St, London and in 1972 the first copy of the lesbian feminist magazine,* Sappho, *appeared. Unlike* Arena 3 *it was produced by a collective who then went on to organise discos and meetings. The magazine folded in December 1981 amd the discos finished in 1982. The meetings continue still and are held every Tuesday at 7.30p.m. at the Victoria, 10A Strathearn Place, London W2.*
5. *See Note 2 after the introduction.*

DIANA CHAPMAN

When I was at school, it was quite common for everybody to fall in love with other girls or staff, so I wasn't peculiar in having tremendous crushes, right, left and centre. But I thought that I'd grow out of it. And I wasn't at all interested in the opposite sex, and the opposite sex wasn't at all interested in me. Then, when I was eighteen, an ex-schoolfriend used to come and see me, I fell in love with her and I thought to myself 'Well, you're still falling in love with girls, you're probably homosexual.' It was all a bit vague. So I suppose I recognised my lesbianism when I was about nineteen, but also I'd been conscious that I was not as others since I was about six. Then I read *The Well Of Loneliness*, and this confirmed me in my belief that I was a lesbian. I even went and bought a copy, it was thirty shillings, which was a lot of money in those days. It swept me off my feet. I identified with Stephen Gordon, and I thought it was tragic and I wept buckets and went around in a daze, for days. I didn't think of it in any literary or critical way, it was far too emotionally powerful for me. It had far too many resonances. I felt a bit religious about it, I think, as though it was something rather wonderful and noble to be. Again, I suppose identifying with Stephen in *The Well Of Loneliness*, I didn't think it was anything terrible, although I realised, of course, that there were enormous disadvantages.

97

Eventually the impact wore off, and then I came to London and I fell in love with somebody else. By this time I was going through a phase where I felt I ought to try and become normal. Of course, everything you read, every psychological book said how immature it was to be homosexual. If there was one thing I didn't want to be it was immature; I thought being immature was terrible. And so I thought probably I ought to take a cure – I ought to get interested in men which I did try to do. I think everybody works through this phase. But it just didn't work, it didn't feel natural going out with a man, on the rare occasions which I did, because I certainly was not knocked down in the rush. It seemed such a false thing. I felt as though I had to behave in a different sort of way because I was with a man. And, there was always the desperate hope that he would invite you out again, and he usually didn't, which left you feeling a total failure. This sort of play did induce feelings of awful failure, because we lived – we still live – in a society in which a woman, especially a young one, is judged very much by her sexual attractiveness. A woman who is seen to be at home every Saturday night, or who can't produce a bloke when there's a dance or something, is stigmatised as a terrible failure. She might be a genius, she might be the greatest sculptor who ever lived, but if she hasn't got a man, what good does it do her? And so, I even went to bed with a couple of men. But even that was 'eeugh'! So men, really, were pretty much a non-event in my life. But I did give it a whirl.

I'm sure that a psychiatrist would have done his or her best to turn me towards accepting the conventional values of what a woman should be like, you know, submissive, child-loving, being prepared to put the man first and to attend to his needs and all the rest of it. Psychiatrists would have tried to turn me into the stereotypical woman. I can't imagine that they would have ever succeeded with me. But there is no question that that's what they would have tried to do.

I was living in Chelsea, and I knew that the Gateways[1] existed, but

I didn't know where it was, and I couldn't find out where it was. Part of me was attracted by the idea, and the other half was repelled. But I used to walk up and down the King's Road looking for tall, handsome women with cropped hair. I just kept thinking they would all be like Stephen Gordon[2] – handsome, well bred and tall, and good at riding. The fact that I wasn't like that didn't impinge. I thought that's what lesbians were like, very, very masculine women. I know why I thought this, because when I was a kid living just outside Bristol, there was a woman called Dora Biggs, who worked for WD & HO Wills, and she was an England hockey player. She was tall, had cropped, smooth-backed hair, and wore men's collars and ties, with a jacket and skirt. My mother always called her, 'That freak Dora Biggs' – so that's how I knew what my mother thought about lesbians. I used to look at Dora Biggs and think 'Oooh' – you know, I found her fascinating.

So I used to trot up and down the King's Road, looking. What I was hoping to see was a whole stream of Dora Biggs look-alikes going down into what I assumed would be the entrance of the Gateways. I didn't know where it was, it wasn't in the 'phone book and I had nobody to ask. Part of me didn't want to go there anyway, I was very ambivalent about it. And I think now, if I had gone there, it might have put me off. It was quite an intimidating place.

I went into hospital to have a hysterectomy in the winter of January 1962. I was convalescing with a friend – this first friend that I had been in love with all those years ago, who was now married. And she brought me a magazine called *Twentieth Century*. In it there was an article by Dilys Rowe called 'A Quick Look At Lesbians'.[3] 'Lesbian' was a word that you never heard mentioned then, and I read the article, which was a load of total cobblers, useless, stupid. So I sat down and wrote a reply – well, it was more of an essay than a letter. The editor wrote back and said 'Do you mind if we publish this?' – and I was absolutely horrified, because I thought 'Ooh, whatever will happen if they publish it? I shall be spat on in the streets, I shall be hauled up before the General Dental Council and struck off, I shall be defrocked.' So, I said 'Yes, all right as long as it's anonymous.'

Then I got a letter forwarded from this Esmé Langley[4] woman. I was in Australia at the time. She said she was starting a lesbian magazine, and there would be a certain amount of stamp-licking, addressing, and that kind of thing – and would I like to help? It sounded as though the magazine was more or less ready to come out! I wrote back and said well, I'd be coming home soon, and yes, I was moderately interested. But again, very ambivalent. I am by nature very timid and I don't like committing myself to anything.

When I got back, to my horror and fury, there was this creature who'd come out to meet the plane, a rather strange figure kitted out in motorcycle gear. This was Esmé Langley. Again, on reading the letter, I'd envisaged something like Dora Biggs – it was nicely typed, and I envisaged some nice, attractive, crisp creature – instead of this, which was totally unlike the picture I'd formed of her and I was furious. Then I had to borrow a pound from her, unfortunately, I only had Australian currency. And so I subsequently met her at a pub in order to return it. It wasn't until Esmé that I met somebody who actually said that they were lesbian. I'd only ever been falling in love with straight women. I did think there weren't many lesbians about, because I had never met any. She was persistent and I, as always, taking the easy way out, went to live with her, not because I was passionately interested in her, but because it saved me looking for accommodation. I was fairly desperate, I'd been living an extraordinary, frustrated life. We lived together for eighteen months, and we did, eventually, after some difficulty, launch *Arena 3*[5] on to a homophobic and unsuspecting public. First of all, it was only a magazine, and a lot of it we wrote ourselves, under different names. I was not only DMC, but I was Elizabeth Godfrey. And Esmé was not only Esmé Langley, she was Hilary Benno. And then one or two people were shuffled along from Anthony Gray, who was connected with the Albany Trust and the Homosexual Law Reform Society –

and, strangely enough, he lived just up the road, which is why Broadhurst Gardens became known as 'Queer Street'. Doreen came along and occasionally she wrote things, as did one or two other people. We found it very difficult to place advertisements but we did manage to in the *Observer* and the *Sunday Times*, and eventually in the *New Statesman*. Gradually more and more people subscribed.

The subscribers started to say, 'Well, this is all very well, reading your magazine. But we want meetings. We want to meet other people.' Esmé and I were a bit reluctant about this – I certainly was, because I'm not very sociable and the idea of meetings rather filled me with horror. However, we decided we'd better give in to this call for meetings. We found a room in a pub called The Shakespeare's Head in Carnaby Street. We couldn't say we wanted a meeting place for a load of dykes, so we muttered something about a meeting place for professional women. The meetings became very popular, and lots and lots of people would come.

There were various debates, and there was a terrible row about turning up in drag. A lot of women – naturally enough – would run home from work, cast off their step-ins, and brush out their perms and sets, and get into gents' natty suitings, and slick down their hair with Brylcream, and turn up looking indistinguishable from young men. And this was rather awkward, because we had to go through the public bar to get up to our meeting room. Of course the chaps at the bar were being told it was women only, and yet there were these seemingly young men trogging up the stairs. It was a bit awkward, and so we said we would prefer it if people didn't wear gents' natty suitings, though of course we didn't mind if they wore jeans and sweaters and things like that. This gave rise to one of our bitterest debates,[6] because people said 'Well, we are repressed and we are oppressed by straight society, and now you are trying to oppress us by not letting us dress as we want to dress.' And we said 'Well, we're not oppressing you, but we are trying to avoid embarrassing situations.' And of course there was a percentage of people who came to those meetings who wouldn't dream of wearing other than the most conventional female attire – twin sets and pearls, things like that. So it was upsetting them when the gents' natty suiting brigade walked in. Whatever we did, we couldn't really win.

We're going back a long way. In those days, the early sixties, one just accepted that there was this butch–femme divide. I never thought of myself as either butch or femme, although people used to try and push me into the butch category, but I never felt that I really belonged there. I didn't feel I belonged in the femme category either. But it wasn't until the women's movement, much later on, that this came out as gender stereotyping, and as such, something which should not be promulgated. It was the beginning of a life within a lesbian circle for a lot of us. A lot of people until then had been living fairly isolated lives, perhaps living with one other person.

Arena 3 was an enormous help in the same way that Sappho[7] was later: people who were living in the country or who thought they were the only person in the world – because you always think you're 'the only person in the world' – suddenly realised that they weren't, and that, in London there were other people like them. In fact, one woman, – a New Zealander – found *Arena 3*, took one look at it, gave up her job, bought her ticket to England and has never returned to New Zealand. It did form a lifeline and for some people, I think it possibly changed their lives.

Later on, in the seventies, I was pleased that things I had been thinking for a lifetime were now beginning to be thought of as part of the women's movement, the whole business of the way women had been subordinated and stereotyped was beginning to be questioned. So I thought the women's movement was an extremely good thing. What I didn't realise, and I think a lot of people didn't realise, and the people in the women's movement didn't realise, is that the women's movement was one thing and lesbianism was another, and the two weren't necessarily the same. We met plenty of lesbians who would say they didn't think much of the women's movement, and, of course, there are thousands in the women's movement who would throw up their hands with horror at the thought that they might be lesbian. Although people say that feminism is the theory and lesbianism is the practice – and I can see the logic of that – nevertheless, the two don't necessarily overlap – although at some points they do. I'm greatly in favour of the women's movement. I honestly don't see how you can be a lesbian and not be in favour of the women's movement. But we do know people who don't regard themselves as particularly feminist. But I think if you're going to live with another woman and spit in the eye of society, and reject the concept that you have to be part of a man, then you have to be feminist. I don't see how you can be anything else.

I don't find it particularly difficult being a lesbian. But I live in London, and I am now very much older and so, therefore, nobody looks at me and says, 'When are you going to find yourself a boyfriend and/or get yourself a husband?' Or, 'Don't you want children?' So the older you get the easier it becomes. I still think that there's awful prejudice, and you have to do a lot of lying by implication. There are a lot of younger lesbians who still dare not tell their parents. Or if they do tell them, get the most dreadful reception – shown the door, 'Never darken our doorstep again' and that sort of thing, which is barbaric. I think lesbianism is still regarded as something very nasty and totally unnatural, which I don't think it is at all. I think it's perfectly natural.

NOTES

1. *See Note 1 after the introduction.*
2. *See Note 1 after Jackie Forster's story.*
3. Twentieth Century, *Winter 1963.*

4. *See Note 3 after the introduction.*
5. *Ibid.*
6. *This debate took place during the summer of 1964 and at the August meeting that year was formally debated through the motion 'That this house considers the wearing of male attire at MRG meetings is inappropriate'. There was a record attendance of seventy members and guests. The voting was almost equally divided. For the motion, twenty-five; against, twenty-eight; abstentions, six.*
7. *See Note 4 after Jackie Forster's story.*

104

BETTY

I remember being always interested in the female hero in pantomimes – the principal boy who was always a girl. I always liked the female stars. At home I was always made to be the boy, the man of the family – girl guide, camping, hiking and biking, I always brought the luggage in. I suppose I wasn't expected to have a boyfriend and I got to feel that that was pretty sissy anyway, and I didn't want that. I don't remember having any sexual attraction to anybody, or at least not recognising it as that until I fell in love at the age of fifty with a woman.

When I got married it was the expected thing to do, and we kidded ourselves we were in love. I only thought of homosexuality in a condemnatory way then. I remember reading a book about a man who grew up a homosexual, and I remember thinking 'Oh, there are some people then who can't help it.' But by and large, I felt that homosexuals should pull themselves together and stop messing about and being nasty. It wasn't a nice thing to be or a nice thing to do. They had, I felt, the power not to be like that. But I didn't really think about lesbians very much. I certainly didn't like the word 'lesbian', and I still don't like it very much. I'm getting acclimatised to it in the last few years, but it's a word I would avoid. I prefer 'gay'.

I was under a lot of pressure to get married. And the right man, or the nice man, the okay man, the one who would be acceptable, came along and we got on very well – a kind of companionship, a sharing of hobbies. He rode a motorbike and so did I; and he liked tinkering about with cars and it was all quite fun, I had to get underneath the car and hold this or do that and get greasy and not worry. I liked wearing old clothes and preferably trousers – not everybody did wear trousers then. And so he liked my company for those reasons. And I suppose we kidded ourselves we were 'in love'. Maybe he was. I know I wasn't, now. For me it was security, it was escape and it was an alternative base to operate from. We were neither of us very awake to any alternatives. We were just doing the expected thing and pleasing our respective mothers, not that I particularly wanted to please my mother, but subconsciously one always does, I suppose – even if we do it in reverse ways. For example, she wanted me to be a doctor, so I became a vet, which was different but it was the same thing, wasn't it? People do marry, people do have two or three children, they do bring them up to be good little heterosexuals and marry when they're twenty, twenty-five, have a couple of kids. And so it goes on and on. I know now that I was simply role-playing, and I was doing it bloody well. So that, at the time, I was really pleased with the way things were going. But I know that inside, I was not alive: I was always tense, I had a lot of physical pain, a lot of stress, a lot of emotional trouble, a lot of psychological stress.

I was feeling very restricted and wanting to do a lot of things that I'd probably conventionally been told that you didn't do once you were past thirty-five or forty. I went to a doctor, who was interested in transactional analysis, and he suggested that I joined a group, which I did. I worked for a year or two in it and that woke me up to alternative ways of being, and accepting myself, and not always being conditioned without question. I began to question things. In that group, there was another woman who was also married with a couple of children. We got into a pattern of going for a walk about once a week to Windsor Park. This went on for several months and I began to get the feeling that there was more to this than met the eye. She had apparently been attracted to me one day and felt herself fall head over heels, but hadn't realised that she was a lesbian, or what was happening. Gradually it dawned on her, and she didn't know how to tell me, didn't know whether I was going to be interested or not, so she went through a certain amount of hell. All the time I was on the wrong wavelength altogether. I suppose one day it suddenly dawned on me – it hit me between the eyes. I thought, 'My God, this is what it must be like! I'm falling in love with this woman.' It was quite devastating.

I wanted to tell everybody that I'd fallen in love. It's really remarkable when I think that my children had probably fallen in and out of love several times by the time I first did. We were shattered when we realised what was happening because we thought we were the only two lesbians who had ever got married and had children. What a mess we had made of our lives, and what the hell were we going to do with it? How were we going to unravel this one? What we didn't realise was it was quite normal, but at that time we panicked. I was working for the Citizens Advice Bureau and I looked up the files under 'homosexuality' when no one was looking – ready to shut them very quickly if anyone came up and said 'What are you looking up?' – and I found a reference to SIGMA[1] which seemed appropriate. They were very helpful to us and understanding. They reassured us that our situation wasn't quite so unusual. We gradually began to realise we weren't alone, though we still didn't know any other lesbians. We read about Sappho[2] in Time Out – we were a bit scared to go along, but we figured we ought to. We started attending there and we've really been linked with Sappho ever since. I helped to run it for a year in 1984 and she took a turn after that. And then of course we really did meet other lesbians, from all walks of life.

We were relieved and very excited, because we could actually be ourselves – particularly in circles where we were with other women. It was a great time. Tuesday nights were not to be missed, because these were the only times, the only two or three hours, that you could really be yourself, and be affectionate with each other, demonstrably so. Nobody raised eyebrows, you didn't have to jump apart if somebody came in the door. There were very few hours that you were able to do this, before you went back into the old acts you had to perform in order to be acceptable. And gradually we found that there weren't just a few people who had done as we had done, being in marriages and then suddenly realising that they were gay – there were thousands and thousands and thousands, and I know now that London is full of women like us, to say nothing of the rest of the world. Certainly in London there are so many people who have either known they were gay and become married or – in a kind of desperation or to cure themselves – have done as we did and conventionally married, and then at some later stage woken up to what they feel they really are. You know, I've learned a whole lot about what it's like, to be a lesbian from all sorts of angles.

After a couple of years, I came out to my husband, which was not an easy thing to do, but it was something I felt I had to, I wanted to do. I couldn't go on living this lie. I told my younger daughter about it, just about the time that my husband and I separated five years ago. It seemed to me to be only reasonable that my daughters should know some of the reasons. My older daughter at that time was more vulnerable, didn't want to discuss anything personal or emotional, but the younger one was different. One evening I was making a cup of coffee and she came into the kitchen. It was about nine o'clock and she said she was off to bed. Her husband had already gone up, and I thought, 'This is the moment, I've got to do it.' And I sort of drew myself up and took a deep breath, and said, 'There's something I really want to tell you, I want to share with you, and it's not easy, and it's . . .'

She said, 'Oh! Go ahead, you know, I'm just going to bed, but that's fine, I'm not in a hurry.'

She made me a cup of coffee, and we stood with our backs against the kitchen units and looked across this space at each other.

She said, 'Well, what's the problem?'

I replied, 'Well, the problem is that if I tell you this it may alter our relationship, and that would be really terrible for me, and I don't know how your husband's going to feel about it either.'

I realised I was building it up into something which was getting her quite scared. I didn't want to do that, so I thought well, come out with it quick. So I said, 'I'm gay.'

And she said, 'Oh, oh, really? Is that all?' Sort of, problem not quite over, but 'I thought it must be worse, I thought you might have cancer or something.'

Then I just started to talk about my fears – I started to cry, because it was kind of a relief that she hadn't rejected it straight away. And she said, 'Well, I had various friends at school who were and, you know, they were fine, and it didn't make any difference to our friendship. So I have a bit of experience about lesbians and I don't find it too shocking, but I'm quite surprised, and, gosh, it must've been difficult for you; and wow, how did you manage?' sort of thing, and I think about an hour and a half later she was still leaning against the kitchen dresser holding a cold cup of coffee. We carried on talking, which felt good. But she still had to tell her husband. I didn't sleep much that night and I was on duty all the next day at the CAB. I pushed off to work before they appeared.

When I got back in the afternoon, I came into the house in some trepidation and, as I came through the door, I sang out 'Hi, I'm home!' They were upstairs – we had an upstairs sitting-room in that house – and there was a kind of thunder on the stairs as my son-in-law came belting down. He gave me an enormous hug and said, 'Hi, Betty! Had a good day?' And again, I burst into tears because I knew he knew, and I knew it made no difference.

At that time I seemed to have been co-operating with the family and fitting in and I didn't see my retirement as being anything different. I was going to go on doing the same old routine which I

109

didn't want to. I learned to jog. I started jogging when I was over fifty. People used to raise their eyebrows and say, 'What, have you always done it?' And I'd say, 'No, I'm just starting.' I started to draw and paint, which I'd never done before. My mother had said, 'You're the scientist. Other people can be artists and do the feminine things. You're the boy, you can go off and do these masculine things. That would please me very much.' That was the message that was coming across, 'I want a son and I haven't got one, and you will do very nicely'. Things like art and music were not what she wanted from me. So it was great fun, I sort of boomed out into the world, drawing and painting and hearing music for the first time, being me, being whole. It felt like an explosion into wholeness. That's probably a contradiction in terms, but it felt very exciting.

In fact, the whole idea of this feeling of love, as I was experiencing it, not just the sexual feelings, but the entirety of love for a woman was something I'd never felt before. I wanted to tell the world. It just seemed so normal and so absolutely ordinary that it wasn't possible to keep quiet about it. And, of course, it was probably quite dangerous to talk to people freely like that, and I've met lesbians since who've said the same thing. It seemed so wonderful and so ordinary, why shouldn't we be accepted? Why should we have to suppress this wonderful thing that's happened to us? That's one of the reasons why I got so upset about Clause 28[3], that, when it's taken people so long to accept their own sexuality, in very difficult circumstances often, a government should come along and suppress you – or at least encourage other people to suppress you, if they don't do it themselves. And to stop you being yourself when it's such a difficult thing to be yourself.

I feel totally accepting of myself now. I know I'm where I need to be, where I am, what is really me is lesbian, and always has been. I know that, looking back, I always was lesbian. And everything else, right through that thirty years of married life, was a role-play.

110

NOTES

1. A support group for the straight partners in couples where the other partner is gay.
2. See Note 4 after Jackie Forster's story.
3. See Note 2 after the introduction.

ROSANNA HIBBERT

I first fell in love when I was fourteen, I think – when I was at school in Kenya. I think I knew it was a rather peculiar thing to do, but I don't know in those days if I ever knew anything about the word homosexual or lesbian or anything like that. I can't remember.

I first started being agonised by it when I was a student in London. I found men very difficult because I'd never had any men in my life. I'd been to a single sex school and I had only sisters, and my father seemed to me, in a curious way, to be a non-person, although he wasn't really. But I agonised about men and my own unacceptability. I suppose I started thinking about lesbianism then, because I remember this curious thing that happened one day. I was on a bus and I saw the woman with whom I'd been in love about six or seven years before. There she was, out of Kenya – suddenly on this bus in the middle of London. It was the most awful experience. First of all, I just felt so awful, because I was wearing such dreadful old clothes, and I wished I was looking nice. I was really shaken up by it. I suppose I was about twenty. That must have set the cat amongst the pigeons in my tiny mind, I imagine.

I've always had problems with my identity. I used to walk round literally thinking I didn't exist. I've always felt affinity towards women, but I haven't labelled it. I haven't always put two and two

113

together that my identity and my affinities with women equalled my being a lesbian. I fell in love with another woman, and I still didn't put two and two together really, not properly.

At one stage I was in love with a woman, I was sharing digs with her – though very little sex, in fact, one might almost say none, really. And then she started going off with men. This was really very difficult and that's when I started looking for psychiatric help – not about being a lesbian, because I didn't know I was, but about not being an actual existing person. But, of course, I now see the two are incredibly, intimately linked. The people I went to see didn't recognise this and therefore, couldn't tell me. At least if they did tell me, they didn't do it clearly enough for me to take it in. I don't think they told me that my identity problem was a sexual identity thing. So for many, many years, I still didn't know that I existed. I still sometimes have problems.

When I was about forty, a lesbian told me I was a lesbian. I needed to be told. I always need to be told things, even if they're as obvious as that. It sounds to me, telling it, an incredible story because it's so stupid. But the basis of it is, my own fear, my own ignorance, my own prejudice. Plus the world's, I suppose.

The first time I went to a *Sappho*[1] meeting, for instance, I didn't know what to expect. I didn't realise lesbians were ordinary people. Oh, I was nervous, because I didn't know what lesbians looked like or what they sounded like or what kind of people they were. I thought, it was . . . almost like going to the zoo to see weird creatures that you've never seen before because you don't live in Southern America or somewhere, you're going to look at all the iguanas or whatever. It was really weird. And, therefore, I didn't know what I ought to look like or I ought to sound like or feel like, or what I ought to do. It was most peculiar. And there I was, getting on for forty. It's mad!

It turned out that I knew, in a funny sort of way – I knew Babs Todd and I sort of knew about Jackie Forster.[2] So it was most

114

extraordinary. I think it was just a great relief to have found some other lesbians.

Fairly soon after that Di and I met, because she was speaking in a debate or something. I always thought that Di[3] was tall, dark and handsome, instead of . . . She wasn't quite as fat in those days . . . certainly dark, but I didn't expect a round face and twinkly round eyes. I expected someone more Radclyffe-Hallesque, I imagine. I don't know why. This was just from reading her articles in *Arena 3*[4]. I suppose it was because she was obviously frightfully important – Esmé made such a fuss in the magazine after Di left. I thought 'She's just got to be this incredibly tall, astonishing person.'

Diana Chapman: I think that people always think we're going to be something wonderful. I mean, if somebody says to you 'Oh lovely, bring her to supper' you're always expecting her to come along with some goddess, and an ordinary little dumpy woman walks in. You think 'My God, is this ordinary little dumpy woman the person they are swooning about?' We always expect goddesses. And it's even worse with men.

Rosanna: We're ruled by stereotypes. Di and I never fell in love with each other or anything. So there was no fundamental fraughtness about it or sort of excitement about it, really.

Diana: No, it just happened, really. No, there was never any throbbing passions or pounding hearts, or that sort of thing.

Rosanna: No, there are other things – but never that. Never that sort of excitement.

Diana: It always sounds as though I've had the most hectic life, one lover after another, and it's not like that at all. I mean, they were pretty well all disasters, and I didn't get much out of them. So it wasn't a sort of joyous, Don Juan-like succession of wonderful escapades. It was just sort of floundering from one rather dreary relationship to another. But it all sounds wonderful when I talk about it, and people think, 'Oooh, what a one she must have been!'

But I haven't been! I've been left bleeding from the ears more than enough times.

Rosanna: I can't remember when I became aware of the women's movement. But I don't see how you can be a lesbian and not be, to one degree or another, feminist. In fact, I sometimes wonder how feminists can not be lesbians, because it's so hard to be connected with men, physically or emotionally and be a feminist. It must be incredibly difficult. So I would suggest lesbianism for everybody, really. It would make the movement very strong! I don't altogether understand all the ins and outs of 'lesbian', 'feminist' and all these other words like 'radical'. I'm never sure what I would be called. I don't want to be called 'right-on' because I don't think that's what I am in so far as I understand that expression. But I don't see how you can be one and not the other.

Lesbianism is the only thing for me though. I think that to come out to somebody, for me, is like a present to a friend. It's not something I do politically. So, for instance, when I was still fully employed, a salaried person, I only told a certain number of people. The people I liked best. I haven't yet got beyond that. I've never been asked to come out as a political gesture. I think I'd probably find it very hard, because it isn't a nice thing to be in the world's eyes. It's getting worse – this backlash. It's also bringing back, or increasing, all these dreadful things like censorship, closing of minds and mouths. It's part of the dictatorship. It's getting harder and harder, I think. I sometimes wonder if I was twenty or thirty now, what I'd do about it. But I don't see what else I could be, however good or bad I am at being it.

NOTES

1. *See Note 4 after Jackie Forster's story.*
2. *Jackie and Babs were co-founders of the* Sappho *collective.*
3. *Diana Chapman – her separate story also appears.*
4. *See Note 3 after the introduction.*

NINA MILLER

I fell in love for the first time when I was six, and I had a relationship with that woman when I was eighteen. She died a couple of years ago at eighty. I think in my teens I was attracted to women emotionally, although I had boyfriends then. I was a late developer in a way, because I didn't have a genital relationship with a woman until I was twenty-seven and I actually had a sexual relationship with a man just before that in the same year. So in a sense, I felt emotionally I'd been in relationships with women, but I read Radclyffe Hall's *The Well Of Loneliness* when I was in my early twenties and one of the things that I hold against that book is that she says women can't make love to each other and, I think, somewhere I believed that. I didn't have the courage to explore for myself.

I enjoyed being attracted to women and had the usual crushes on teachers and that sort of thing – and certainly when I got to know this teacher again, she gave me a great deal of affection and I respect her because she didn't seduce me, and she could have done. So that was a great bonus in my life really. A lot of gentleness and kindness.

I knew from when I was six that my mother was jealous of her – so I was fairly careful about what I talked about with my mother, and there was some point when I was eighteen when my mother tried to stop me seeing her. Looking back, I realise that, because of the way

119

she talked to me about them, my mother was trying to put me off lesbians. But I didn't associate it with how the woman and I were. So I heard the information and didn't like it, but my affection with the friend was something different, which was a good thing.

There were two role models for me in Jersey when I was young. There was a woman who lived on the beach near us who was very tall and thin, and a very strong swimmer. She saved a number of lives. She lived right on the edge of the beach and she used to swim out and drag people back. And she wore men's suits and had an Eton crop. An Eton crop was the thing in the thirties so that was a 'legal' hairstyle. I picked up that there was something 'iffy' about her. It was rather funny because I think I quite admired her as a child. I asked questions about her because she was different. I thought it was very romantic – dashing out to sea and dragging people in. She must have started doing this when I was quite young. She'd probably be in her twenties or thirties then.

There was another woman who was the cashier at a very 'nice' restaurant in the town. She again wore men's pinstripe suits. She sat in one of those things – I think they call it a *caisse* in French – behind a mahogany counter. So presumably the trousers weren't seen in the day. How she got away with that in Jersey – pre-War – I do not know. It was a respected job and she lived in the village where I was born. Again, there was no conversation about her. If I asked about her, I picked up that she was 'iffy' and I was very curious. It was awkward in that those were the only role models – I wouldn't have known a feminine lesbian from anyone else. I didn't realise that women could be feminine and love other women.

So those were the role models that I had. I knew that I didn't fit them. I didn't particularly want to be like that. The two roles that I was offered were being feminine and doing the things one was supposed to do to attract boys. And these other women were rather what I suppose I'd call butch women now. And I don't think I wanted to fit either of them.

120

I spent quite a lot of time when I was young thinking I was a boy. But not quite. I knew I didn't want to be the kind of feminine woman my mother wanted me to be. I read adventure books and identified with the boy heroes. Another kind of choice was between being a woman and being a man. So certainly I spent some time being butch. Then I think I found my own middle road after that. I would have been shy of talking to anyone about it. When I did my teacher training in London, there were only five of us in a small group and three of us were lesbians, which, looking back now, I think, 'Wow, what a bonus!' We were all much too shy then; I was apparently being pursued by one of them without realising it and got together with the other one. I was so naive!

When I qualified as a teacher – there was a period when I was living on my own when I was about twenty-two or twenty-three, and I remember going to the public library and hunting for books and reading what I could find. I read several of Radclyffe Hall's books and they were on the stack – you had to actually go up to the desk and ask for them, which was a bit embarrassing. I read Freud when I was in my twenties, it was *Three Essays Towards a View of Sex* where he said he thought most people were bisexual. I found that quite comforting because it didn't say I was deviant. The other books I'd read implied that there was something wrong, it was a sickness. And so I tended to look for answers to *why* was I a lesbian, for a while.

I probably felt guilty and worried and felt it was something I had to pretend about in some way. I think I always knew that if somebody confronted me, I wouldn't deny it. On the other hand, I didn't have the courage just to be out and say 'That's how I am.' So I tended to have single relationships. I met somebody when I was training as a teacher – I had a third year in London – we were in a sexual but not genital relationship. Fairly closeted, really. That's one of the things I find painful to look back on – I realise now that I was quite afraid then. It would have been an awful shock to me if the first woman I loved had actually made love to me. I was quite prejudiced

121

in a way – I thought it wasn't normal. It took me some years to accept same-sex love. And thinking about it – I used to find it really hard to accept male gays – the idea of men making love to each other. I used to say to myself 'Look, if you love your own sex, why can't they love theirs?' I found that hard to take in. Somehow over the years, I then arrived at the fact that it was all right to be me. I don't know how it came about.

I found other lesbians slowly. I suppose you deduced that somebody was a lesbian: they're not married; they don't have a boyfriend; they live with another woman. You got to know someone enough until it was fairly obvious that you were both fond of each other. Then one or another of you had the courage to do or say something. A slow process! It's more lively and open these days.

I had two fairly long relationships – five and seven years. I lived in serial monogamy then. I was just in my little furrow and didn't think the world could be different. I suppose that kind of loneliness was fairly characteristic of anybody who didn't know where the "scene" was or hadn't got contacts through *Arena 3*[1] or *Kenric*,[2] which would have been going then. So I only knew the women I lived with or – say – their ex-partners or my ex-partners. I didn't have a lot of choice. So I made relationships with people who were there. It's funny. It was a bit like living underground – it was a lack of awareness – of being lonely and not knowing that there was a world we could join. I didn't get on to the scene until I was in my forties. So I didn't know anything until about twelve years ago, when I was living with a woman and we knew no other lesbians except some woman we weren't that keen on. We decided that this was a bit silly, that we actually were quite lonely. My partner sent off for a copy of *Gay News* and from there we learned about *Sappho*, which had weekly meetings in London. I remember the first night I went there, I sat with my back to the wall and I looked around the room and I was absolutely amazed. I thought if you'd gone along Oxford Street and taken one woman in every ten, you'd have that range of women there.

I'd got no idea so many different women were lesbians. And that was really nice.

This led on to other things, like getting in touch with *Sequel*[3] and they had a monthly supper together in a public restaurant. They arranged walks sometimes. I discovered there was a local gay group in Essex called Octopus and the Quaker group called the Friends Homosexual Fellowship – which was a mixed group. So my social life widened out enormously after that.

Later I think the push probably came from me to start coming out in our private life. The first two women we shared that with just shrugged and said 'Yes, we've always known.' So we felt a bit silly about pretending about having separate bedrooms and things. Another friend didn't mind at all. I don't think we had one awkward reaction, which made us feel much more comfortable. I was more at ease with myself after that. We used to go away, for instance, at Christmas with a straight friend who didn't know. So we spent that holiday time pretending that we weren't lovers. Seems silly.

I gradually came out completely in my private life. By the time I was a head teacher, most of my social life was gay. I didn't come out at work because I thought that was dangerous. I was closeted all my teaching career. I was out in my private life for at least six years towards the end of my career. First of all, I didn't think I could cope with the war of nerves. If the parents decided they didn't like a lesbian headmistress, it would have been quite a battle. I was a head teacher in a junior school – the staff knew but I didn't say I was a lesbian. That was a piece of thought out strategy on my part, because I decided that if ever there was a 'hoo-ha' about it, and parents can have witch hunts about such things, then it would be up to them to *prove* that I was a lesbian. I wasn't going to give them that ammunition. I had also thought out what I would do if that happened. I asked a friend of mine who was a heterosexual woman, well up in counselling – if she would come and support me at a public meeting. She said she would and, having made that strategy, in a way

I relaxed and thought 'Well, I've covered myself.' I thought my aim would be to go down fighting. I didn't think I'd survive the pressure if there were a group of parents saying 'We want this head out.' Technically, I couldn't have been sacked for it. But the nervous pressure, the stress to face one of those situations would be pretty hard to imagine. So I wasn't going to give anybody that weapon against me.

I came across gayness once with a parent who was gay and losing access to a child, and I think that parent was very surprised I was sympathetic. That's really the only way it touched school and parents. I used to feel as I walked through the door that I was leaving part of me outside the building each day, and that was one reason why I wanted to come out of teaching. My private life was completely out by then, and I almost felt that I was going back in the closet each time that I walked into the school building. I really wanted to be in a life where I was my own boss. I wanted to be completely out.

I was a fairly strong woman in a way. I was the only woman head in that area. There were five junior schools, four were run by men and I got my job in competition against four or five men, though they'd had a woman before me and one after me. I discovered after I left from a teacher I kept in touch with, that the staff knew I was a lesbian. I came out to her after I'd left. We discussed it. She'd turned up at school one day dressed in a man's suit with a tie – when that was fashionable – and somebody said to me, 'You ought to wear that sort of outfit.' And I said, 'No thanks, I'd look too butch.' And I just left it at that. But I thought 'Oh, they don't miss much, but I don't want to look like Radclyffe Hall, thank you.' So when I left work, I was out altogether, which was a relief.

I've always chosen to live in towns, because it's much easier to be anonymous. I wouldn't want to live in a small village. I tend to be completely out, somewhere safe, like a Quaker meeting. I recently went on an embroidery course at the Embroiders Guild headquarters

124

and I didn't come out there. That was quite a change for me, because I generally look for opportunities to be out if I'm in classes. It's part of my quiet campaigning: I think it's very good for people to discover, to be confronted with what you might call 'perfectly ordinary lesbians' – that we're just part of the population. They'll get to know me, and when it's appropriate I'll say 'No I don't live with a man, I have a woman lover.' And there'll be a little silence and then they'll probably start talking quite happily. If you give people an opportunity to know more about a situation, then they'll take that on board and start thinking what they're up to.

I think Section 28 has given people permission to be prejudiced. It's like when you've got the National Front around – people think it's OK to be racist. I think it's a similar thing for us going on now. My first reaction to the Clause 28[4] was that I was not willing to go back in the closet, and that if we ever have to go on in an underground way, then we need to build up networks. I think women are very good at it, and have always done it. Women have friendships in a way that men don't.

I think I've taken a much harder look at what goes on in the world – how men have the power and the money and so on. I see women as really fulfilling a service role – women service men in many senses. I don't put energy into men. The places where I meet them are in Quakers, in counselling training and in my shared house. I don't knowingly put energy into men in anything but those places, where I will also confront them. Since I've retired and finished counselling training I only work with women. I want to choose where I put my energy now. I think that's probably the influence that feminism has had on me.

Looking back on my early life, it seems to have been very lonely as I rarely knew more than the lesbian I was living with. Maybe one other. I actually counted up the other day to see how many I knew now, and it's at least sixty acquaintances or close friends. So it's a big change. I thoroughly enjoy life now. It's great. I feel very relaxed.

125

Most of my life is orientated around women, I work with women now and I imagine about eighty or ninety per cent of my social life is with lesbians. I've got access to books. It wasn't until relatively recently, about seven years ago, that I started reading feminist books. I found that very affirming because it made sense of my experience as a woman. And I was very pleased to discover that I could read specialist areas – in the last year I've read a lot about women and spirituality. I found there is a whole movement within the women's movement which is particularly concerned with that. So it's been very comforting to find those threads. Sometimes I go to films, women's classes and women's holidays. That's very satisfying.

There's a lot more knowledge around now. I wish there had been more lesbian books and information about sexuality when I was younger, and access to other women who were lesbians. I don't think it's necessarily easier now. Young lesbians, who are more visible, get cat-called, which I didn't when I was young, and still face prejudice from workmates, parents and friends. They are physically at risk and can lose their jobs. I think the main change is in the spread of information and more open networking. Certainly I'm glad that a lot more knowledge is available for me.

NOTES

1. *See Note 3 after the introduction.*
2. *See Note 1 after Sylvia's story.*
3. *Sequel was an organisation which helped isolated and lonely lesbians. It is no longer in existence.*
4. *See Note 2 after the introduction.*

DOROTHY DICKSON-BARROW

As far back as I'm aware of my sexuality, or sex, I realised that I was a lesbian. So I would say it was when I was at boarding school, between the ages of twelve and fourteen. I suppose it was like any other boarding school – the crushes you have on teachers there. You're aware of that issue. You didn't give it a name, or at least I don't think I gave it a name. I felt it was just natural; just nice to be with women that you like and I think we saw it as fun, too. I mean, we knew there was some vigorous secrecy about not doing certain things – sort of kissing each other when other people were around, but I'm not even quite sure we did a lot of that. It was very much feelings and emotions that were important in those days. Perhaps I got the feeling that I liked a certain person, and when I was about thirteen or fourteen Radclyffe Hall's book, *The Well Of Loneliness*, came out. I presume a lot of women of my age found it as their Holy Bible, or something like that. When you read that, it gave you some identity about what it was you were feeling. I really realised there was some labelling then, to who I was. And that was important, that "Gosh"! For the first time I knew what liking women was, what this feeling you are getting was all about. I think the thing that attracted me to the book was the picture of Radclyffe Hall. And I used to fancy myself looking like this woman, you know, with the cravat and white shirt and tie. You had to keep this book a secret you see because it was banned from publication.[1]

I was brought up in a middle-class structure at home and, therefore, could identify with some of the things in the book. I had two brothers and I can remember envying them, wanting to dress like them, to look like them and to have the sort of freedom of being able to climb trees. So I don't think I saw it so very much as different from my own life in a certain way.

I knew that women fascinated me, I knew that my Maths teacher and my Latin teacher were absolutely fantastic, that I would do any amount of work for them. But I also knew that I adored my brothers and my father. I just wanted to do the things they did because I felt, even as a small child, how much more exciting boys' things were than girls' play. For instance, they played with electric trains, they played tops. We used to call it 'pics' at home, in Jamaica. They flew kites, they did all the exciting things that girls didn't do because girls dressed up in frilly dresses. I can remember my mother feeling very desperate, because she had this one daughter that she wanted to dress up. I was brought up in the days when Shirley Temple pictures were around, so I grew up with Shirley Temple curls and 'damsel' dresses with big bows. It was awful for me because I just didn't want to look like that. I can remember once or twice going on the barbed wire fence and ripping my dress. My grandmother discovered what I was doing and patched it, so I could still wear it, you know, that sort of thing. So you reach the stage where you know you're not going to win, but you still want to do the things that one's brothers did, because they were much more exciting.

I think most of us at boarding school had some sort of crush on somebody. And it was a kiss and a cuddle. It's interesting – it wasn't a physical relationship you had with people. It was talking, it was like having a mentor, it was like wanting to be with somebody, being moved by them spiritually because I think at that age sexuality was very much "thinking", that it is a feeling you have and you don't act

128

on the feeling. You want that deep friendship and it's very spiritual. And you didn't put the physical connotation to it, except occasionally you would have a cuddle.

Acting on my feelings happened much more when I went into nursing because I was older, and so, therefore, one's awareness of sex was there. Whilst you're at school, the awareness of it is a different sort of thing – it was much more a crush syndrome or something like that. But once you got into nursing, there was more discussion around sexuality and feelings, of putting action to the feelings and so forth. And there were a number of us around. It amazes me when I hear my Black brothers and sisters talk about 'It's a white person's disease, it doesn't happen among us.' I'd love to tell them to go back to my days as a nurse in Jamaica, 1953 to 1956. There were a significant number of Black women who were lesbians and Black men who were gay.

So it was quite fun, it was quite an important period in my life. The thing about it in those days – I still don't think that I put a label to it – it was just that you preferred the company and the intimacy of women. But the first time I actually had a physical contact with somebody I thought it was something out of heaven. It was good, and it was beautiful and it was sensitive and very caring, and quite explosive really.

In those days, I think most of us lived in two worlds. One world was for one's family and one's community, and the other world was very private, where you met with your friends, you had your dinner parties. And you dressed accordingly: to suit your family, to suit society. But at home in the evenings, you dressed in slacks. And you'd even imitate my mentor, which was to dress in cravats – dinner wear, tails, making sure your shirt, the blouses you wore had cufflinks, and various things like that. Then as I got older, I can remember starting to smoke pipes or cigars. So there was a pseudo-imitation of your mentor, who was Radclyffe Hall in those days. There was an external behaviour and an internal behaviour, which was in private. That was the pattern, I think, for a lot of people. There were some who dressed

129

like that all the time, but others of us had some sort of pressure, or felt that our family would disapprove. It was important that at no stage did our behaviour pattern affect our relationship with the family and their life in society.

I think my family knew, or they suspected; they used to think of it as Dorothy and her abnormal friends, or Dorothy and her abnormal behaviour, Dorothy with her peculiar friends. And, to a certain extent, some of those friendships were encouraged to be dissolved, or you were encouraged not to pursue them. It was not the fact of being friends with women that was wrong, because that was a common thing. In every society and every culture there is always a very strong move to be friends with women. But if they had any inclination that it was anything further than that, then that would be seen as abnormal. So, as far as the family was concerned, no, I never ever told them. Not my parents, nor my relatives.

When I came to England, in 1957, there was a very small group of us who didn't have to come. We came for further, higher education or to take a post-graduate course or something. A number of us, men and women, stayed for a good while and we spent a lot of time together. So, to a certain extent, my life changed, and I got married and had children. I think you got married in those days because it was expected of you and there was the whole thing about not having sex outside marriage. So, if you had sexual feelings, you thought you had to get married. So I think it was a whole social pressure being put on you. And as you get older I think you feel that that's what life is about, getting married. I also think there was something in my subconscious that felt that if I got married, these sexual feelings about women would go. And, you realise after you get married, it doesn't go, it's still there.

The moment I got married it was a total disaster. But even then, my husband was very good. I mean he immediately realised where I was. But what was even more interesting is that this girl I started to have a relationship with actually told him about my sexuality. So, that he knew and although I wouldn't say accepted it, he didn't reject it – it was 'Oh, well, this is something that happened then'. But when you go through this you realise something isn't right. Then my husband died when my younger daughter was nine months old.

It was ages after, and I was quite depressed and really felt for the first time that I wanted to talk to somebody about my feelings, my sexuality. And I spoke to a friend of mine who had known me from before the girls were born. And I remember how supportive she was. She wasn't a lesbian, but was always very supportive throughout her life.

About that time I met another woman. I can remember her sitting down on the floor in her living room talking in this lateral way about books, and Radclyffe Hall came up. And she'd read her! And I can remember how the spark flew between us and that was the beginning of the first relationship I could really label as a sexual one. She was the sort of person who gave me meaning to what it was all about. It just escalated into a very intensive three years of a relationship which, as intensely as it started, was as intensely as it stopped. Because she was married, she had children, and she wanted security. She moved up to Nottinghamshire and I decided that this was the woman of my life. I thought I'll get a job up in the North, so I moved. And that didn't work out. Soon after she realised she didn't want this. Her son, as a matter of fact, discovered some letters and then told his father; and I think the father threatened her that if she didn't give this up, he would expose the whole situation. So I think this was quite painful for her, and she decided she would finish with me. I'm sure a lot of people would find it hard to understand her going back to stay with her husband. But what could I offer her in the early sixties, you know? And so she remained with her husband. I think it's one of the problems for a lot of people of my age who did like women, and who were married – what could you do? She didn't have the security at that time; she didn't have a career; she was a mother of five children. It's only after he came out of the army that she did a course in nursing and was able to have her independent life. But by that time, we had actually made our different paths. But it had been quite an enriching situation.

I think that's the sort of thing that I would say happened to a lot of women of my age range or older. That, unless you remained a nurse or a teacher (although in those days, you couldn't get married in those professions anyhow, so it didn't matter) no other women unless you were middle class, had financial security. I'm sure the nursing and teaching professions were full of women who shared lives together in a very obscure way.

So I drifted. And then I related to a man for twelve years, who was a very gentle, caring person. By that time I'd had my children, bringing them up on my own, and we had a very close, loving and caring relationship. And I struggled, through all that time I still struggled with my lesbianism. There were times when I tried to bring this subject up with him – to say, 'Look, you know, this is me.' It's only after we broke up that he actually put two and two together. I mean, it was quite interesting – I had a year out and met a lot of lesbians, people who are friends now in Leeds. They were very supportive, you know, whilst I was going through this very difficult time. I was very depressed over it, because I kept thinking 'What are you going to tell your daughters? How are you going to handle this?'

As my children grew up, and I became much more involved with the politics of race, and my socialist politics, I found more and more of the lesbians that I mixed with were white. They gave me a tremendous amount of support round my sexuality. If I'm depressed, if something breaks up, there they are. So I was getting my support from my white lesbian friends – but I was also in the whole politics of race, where the people I was fighting were also white people. Moving more and more in the area of race, there's a tremendous conflict, because my sexuality doesn't play a part in my work round race. Or I haven't allowed it to play a part. And there's a conflict there, because race is important and then you suddenly find that your sexuality has to be hidden. Not that I don't think my sexuality is important, but I think I am me, and I don't see why my sexuality has to be addressed. Neither do I expect it to be denied but I have to deny it within the political area in which I move round race, and the Black community because I'm not quite sure that the Black community, except the ones who are lesbians themselves, would give me that support. I haven't put it to the test, and therefore it's difficult to know, but it is a conflict. For me, it's like the whole notion of . . . where white people often will say to me 'You're OK, it's the others', I think the same thing would happen in the Black community, that they would say 'You're OK, but it's the others.' Those two arenas are difficult strands to walk because both bring in an element of tolerance, and I believe there's an intolerance in that tolerance, and that's a conflict. But also it's older women because I think there is a difference between how older lesbians relate. I can only talk about the ones I know myself, I think most of us of my age, have been lesbians but have become feminists later on, whereas most modern lesbians that I know have come into lesbianism from feminism. And I think there is a difference, in our approach, in our philosophy, in our thinking, our reaction, and all these things.

So I think, in meeting my new lover – it's not new, it's a number of years now – it's a learning process for both of us. Because she's got to learn what it is like to relate to somebody Black, and somebody Black who is political, and who will come home and be very angry about what society is doing out there to Black people. And I then have to learn from her, and actually have to listen and hear some of the difficulties she experiences, relating to a Black woman; knowing of the racism that I experienced there. But you can't live with that and take it to bed, or take it to breakfast, or take it to lunch, or take it to anything all the time because you'll never survive. So, there's a beauty in that sort of relationship, there's a strength in it – it's never boring, it's not only the context of two people from two different cultures relating, but two people relating from two different age ranges. And so you get another dimension within that relationship. That's quite exciting.

When I started this relationship with my present lover, I had to decide how do you tell your children? I remember the first Christmas. I decided I wasn't going to have a family Christmas. I was a bit down before all this so I announced to my daughters that they had to look after themselves – they were grown up; one was married and had a child, and the other one was living away. The one with the child, decided to come to see me because she knew something was on my mind, and she wanted to talk to me about it. I always remember that weekend. I'd never hoovered a house so often, because she kept sort of pressing that we have this discussion about other people coming out. And then she suddenly looked at me, and she said 'Well, when are you coming out?' And I sort of switched the hoover on and moved it around!

Eventually I had to tell her. And, it was good. She said, 'Well, I knew for ages, I was just waiting for you to say.' Because while she was with me, she had another friend who came to see her, and she went walking with her, and said, 'You know, I think my mother is a lesbian, but she doesn't know how to tell me.' So that was rather nice. And she was very supportive. I asked this daughter not to tell my other daughter yet, and I decided that after Christmas, I would arrange to see her and tell her. And again, I went around the mulberry bush for ages with her, till eventually I told her. And then, she came up and said, 'Well, I knew.' And then she started to talk, to think of all the people that she knew used to come to the house that she thought I had a relationship with – none of them, I mean, I didn't. But the fact is that they were always aware that I was different from other mothers and loved me even more for that, because there wasn't a pattern of conventional behaviour, in the house. So, they were very supportive, they were quite positive about it. What their worry was wasn't for themselves nor for their immediate partners. I think what

134

they were worried about were the friends of their friends – how would *they* deal with it?

I think for me, lesbianism has been positive in that way. I feel much more pain these days because when you're private with it, it's very easy to stay within your four walls and lead your private life in isolation. But because I have another life, which is a political life, how do you mix those two things together? And that's a problem, not only for myself as an older lesbian, but for myself as an older Black lesbian, who has taken a political stance nationally and locally. It's extremely difficult. So, therefore, you're torn between these two things all the time. You're also torn as an older person – and I suppose as a younger person – and my relationship with somebody white. So you walk that tightrope the whole time. So, yes, it has its difficulties. And I suppose as an older woman who is a lesbian, what does my daughter say to her children? What do you say to your grandson? That grandmother is funny, is different? She's going to have to find – I can't do it for her – she's going to have to find the language to use and the positive things to give. I think this is one of the dilemmas, I find, as a grandmother.

I didn't like being a grandmother at the beginning. I adore it now, I think my grandson is marvellous, and I wouldn't be without him. And I hope he'll grow up to be quite sensitive, and accepting me, of who I am. What I want is that if people discover that I am a lesbian, or if I should share that with people, I expect them to respect that and respect me as they did before. That is not to say I want to stand up on the hilltops and shout about it. What I want is that if my colleagues and my friends and my acquaintances know that I am a lesbian, I want them to treat me the same as they would treat anybody else. I want people to recognise that I am who I am, and who I am happens to be a lesbian, happens to be a mother, happens to be a grandmother, happens to be a lover, happens to be a professional worker – all those sort of things.

I think feminism had an effect on my lesbianism in that it gave me

135

a lot more courage to do things, a lot more courage to be much more open. Because, I think, for women of my age, there were two worlds, for us – the private world, and the public world. And to a certain extent, that still does happen. I think this is the evil of society – that a whole group of people have to live two lives. Now, I believe feminism has given me, or helped me, or given just that extra little thing to me which says, 'You are you. And be proud of who you are.' It has also confused me. Because you take more risks, where I think it was safer to live in the two worlds . . . the private world, and the public world. I think the risk you take of trying to open that door and let that light in, moves you into a different arena, and I'm not quite sure it's always easy to live comfortably anymore. So feminism has created a great discomfort, and the reason why you're experiencing that discomfort is the fact that you've opened that door, and you've let that light in, and you have no control over it. It then becomes much more difficult to hide or to have that private world anymore.

I know I am taking a risk of that door being opened. But I do believe, that at some stage in one's life, one has got to – or I have got to say, that you can no longer survive and feel comfortable with those around you if you can no longer walk and hold your head high. It's quite an interesting thing – as a child, my mother taught me that, because I'm short, I should always walk high with my head tall, to look tall and to feel tall. And yet still, there's part of my life that I haven't walked tall, because I haven't been able to say who I am, because, you see, your sexuality tells you who you are. There's something about owning that inner self, and exposing that inner self. Because sometimes when the light is in your eyes, and the smile, and all those other things that happen, people think, 'Gosh! You're so extrovert, you're so this and that.' They don't know what's underneath that gives that sort of look, that gleam in your eyes. So, yes, being in this film you take your risk, you open that door. But you reach a stage in life where you have to make that decision. And that's where feminism has given me that hope, but that strength too, to open that door.

The problem for me as a Black woman is that I see my feminism differently from white feminists, because I've come to it from a different angle. It's very difficult, because I think white feminists have had, to a certain extent, a luxury, to sit back and to think and to work out a philosophy. I remember reading Bell Hook's *From Margin To Centre* when she talked about white women having the luxury of being feminist, of liberation, because they were able to have Black women to work in the houses, and clean and look after the children.

Now, I think it's the same thing with working-class women in this society. Working class women live in a much more enclosed environment. Middle class people can move – they're more mobile. So if you want to be a lesbian, you can move from the area. You can go to university, and then you'll have more mobility to get jobs elsewhere. The working-class woman is very much inside – I mean, both a closer environment, and a much more claustrophobic environment. And, therefore, it's much more difficult to be a lesbian and to be private. And I think sometimes, that's why some of them, actually, blow it, and say they can't handle it. And I think those sorts of things are difficult, because it's just like being a Catholic, or it's like being a Black woman. I think it's for the same reason that some Black women find it difficult to come out, and will always be in the closet as lesbians, because the environment is much more claustrophobic, it's much more on top of you.

I was at a conference recently, where I met a number of younger Black lesbians. They really thought, or at least my perception was, that lesbianism started with them. They were shattered, or quite amazed that there was somebody with grey hair who was their mother's age, perhaps their grandmother's age, who is a lesbian and always has been.

I think people of my age have had to work pretty hard. We haven't had that time to sit back. Because not only is the fight out there enormous, as a Black person, but when you see some of the things that white feminists are sitting back and thinking – for instance, they will say you're a traitor if you want to do certain things with men and so forth. It's not easy, because as far as I'm concerned, my race, my colour, comes first, my gender is next. Now many feminists think that's a load of crap, but I think, in reality people see my colour first before they see my gender. And in this society, I have to fight with Black men, because when the enemy comes, they're not going to put me aside with my white feminist friends and say 'We won't attack you, because you're a lesbian or you're a feminist with these white feminists.' They see me first as a Black person. So, for me, that's one of the differences I have to face with my white feminist friends. I also think that my experience and my age range have created different problems. I'm also saying to white feminists that what they say, often, isn't always right, or isn't applicable to me as a Black woman. It may be right for them, but it's not right for me as a Black person.

As an older lesbian – and I'm sure other older lesbians you've spoken to – I bet you all of them, without fail, will say it was never an easy road, and never will be an easy road. For me to have survived, I've had to leave home. I've never been back. And I'm sure part of my not going back is the fact of who I am, and I know that if I went back, I could no longer pretend.

I would like to say to younger lesbians, 'Don't just condemn us for not coming out. But recognise that within each decade, there is different social behaviour, and different codes of behaviour, whether you like it or not.' Because you're part of that society, you have to follow that, or else you're going to live a very lonely life. And I don't know what my life would be like now if I had come out openly many years ago. I don't know. I'm not going to put it to the test. I know now I feel more comfortable to take this risk. I think once you actually acknowledge where you are, sexually or politically, you take risks. Because you're challenging the *status quo*. So, therefore, it becomes a much more difficult and rough road to go through. On the other hand, all challenges are exciting, and as you get older, you haven't got much more to lose.

NOTES

1. The Well of Loneliness *was banned in 1928 and described in the press of the day as 'a story of perverted lives' and 'nauseating'. It was not republished in this country until 1948, by Falcon Press.*

JAN RUSSELL

From quite a young age I was always very attracted to the women I worked with. I always had ideas and fantasies about spending time with them other than in the office. It's embarrassing to think about it now. I did ask somebody to go away with me on holiday once, to my sister's place in the country, but it wasn't very relaxing really, because I felt quite attracted to her and I think she was aware of that so she spent a lot of time trying to keep me away. And my sister was having marriage problems, so it wasn't really a very comfortable place to be. That was the only time I asked anyone away until I was with Mary – and then we spent all our time together – all our holidays together.

I was nineteen. Our relationship lasted for two years when we were nursing in New Zealand. We were in the same year and I admired her tremendously. We came from similar backgrounds and got on very well together. One day I just went into her bedroom – we used to visit each other after we'd come off the wards – and suddenly it all came out. I can't remember what we were talking about, but we ended up saying that we were both very attracted to each other, liked each other very much and that was it, the start of it. It was conducted in great secrecy. Nursing was very strict then: lights out at eleven o'clock. So there were creepings, from one door to another; we weren't the only ones creeping around, but we thought we were the only ones creeping around for the specific purpose of spending the night together. And that's what we used to do at home; our parents thought we were just good friends and didn't think it was at all strange that we shared a bed together. People were always dropping in, visiting each other and it wasn't really out of the ordinary for girls to sleep together in shared beds. I think actually in New Zealand it was quite a common thing to do, so they probably didn't think about it very much. We were very good friends and used to go to all the family gatherings together, spend all our time together. Her parents were quite well off and they used to lend us a car and caravan for holidays. So we had quite a good time, really. It was quite stressful when we broke up – it was more stressful for me, in a way, because I was having a lot of skin problems. Shortly afterwards I decided to give up nursing because I had very bad hands – they used to come up in a rash. So I had two big upheavals at one time. She had decided she wanted to go and live with this bloke who she eventually married and she had seven children and is still married to him.

I suppose I just felt it was going to go on for us both and when it ended – quite devastatingly for me – I just went the way a lot of other women went – back to heterosexuality and on from there.

I came to England in 1956. I spent six weeks on ship and met other women on the way over. Six of us got together and set up a flat. The same thing happened – I got crushes on them, but didn't do anything about it.

I left New Zealand when I was twenty-two and married when I was twenty-five – I just thought there was something wrong with me, because I still kept getting these crushes. But I put it aside and I thought that when I got married it wouldn't happen again. I didn't really think about it, it was always there but I didn't really try to explore it. I just kept feeling attracted to women and not doing anything about it.

I was monogamous, I was never attracted to other men. Life was a

142

struggle. I was pregnant when we married, and he didn't have any money or anywhere to live and that's what the first ten years were about really: having children, trying to survive, moving out of London to Luton, living there for sixteen long years and the first ten were just a survival experience really.

I got married partly because I was pregnant, but I also quite liked him – for a man, he was quite considerate. I was also having epileptic fits and he was quite considerate about that. I think it was also about feeling isolated in London, and also being frightened about the fits which were quite serious. And he was kind to me.

After the children had got to school, I started to work again, and I began to meet other women. Then I started playing badminton and I met a lot of other women, I can think of one woman I was very attracted to at the time, but we were very different. She was quite well off, she lived in a private housing section of Luton, and we lived in council housing. Really very different backgrounds. But we got on well together on certain levels, played badminton and spent a lot of time together. Then I met another woman and was really very attracted to her and I think she knew but she didn't want to do anything about it. It was then I realised I'd got to make some decisions.

My daughter had gone to college by the time I left – I'd already told her I was probably going to leave and why. The boys I didn't talk to and I think that was wrong of me, because I went to college for two years and they thought I was just going to college, not leaving home. It just got too difficult going back and I ended up not going there. I think at the time I realised I'd just got to think about myself, because if I'd thought about anyone else too much, I just wouldn't have done it. It was the first time in my life I was entirely selfish. That was 1980 and I was forty-six years old.

I get on very well with my children now, though I don't see much of them. They know I'm a lesbian, it's no problem. I didn't enjoy college much – quite an intense two years. I had an affair while I was there which didn't work out. There were quite a few older lesbians there – very closeted – it was quite a difficult time. It was a women's college, but feminism might never have existed.

On the whole, I feel happy, and lucky. I've had a few problems healthwise, but I used those two years to build up contacts and the Older Feminist Network (OFN) started and I started with it and then eventually we moved on to the Older Lesbian Network (OLN). I've always had a lot of younger lesbian friends, and I think that's because I came out in the women's movement and my politics were more those of a younger woman. I didn't really feel the gap until I was fifty, but when I had my fiftieth birthday, I went away for six months and it was the first time I'd ever done anything on my own. It made a big difference to me.

I think I'm lucky that I have children. I agree with lesbians who've always been lesbians who say that being married gives you some sort of protection, it does. And having children, even if you're a lesbian, gives you some sort of different identity.

It was twenty-nine years before I went back to New Zealand. I went back a different person. My brother said 'We've got a surprise for you later on.' I began to feel instant tremblings and worry and fear, and I really had no idea what surprise my brother could have for me because I'd already decided, though we'd been close as children, we'd grown apart and had very little in common any more. Then somebody knocked on the door and he looked up with a big smile on his face and he said, 'Oh, this is the surprise.' He went to open the door and I heard this woman's voice. It took a minute for it to register, and then I just ran into the hallway and it was this woman I had been involved with. She looked very much the same, though older, but hadn't really changed much at all. We were both really pleased to see each other again. It was very difficult sitting through that half hour, like a dream, with the family thinking we were just good friends, and me thinking about that time, and her thinking about it.

But I think she tumbled quite quickly to where I was at. I did go and visit her a couple of times. Her family had all grown up. She'd had seven children and I was quite overwhelmed by that fact although I'd had three. They were all very tall and well built; she'd had four sons and three daughters, and I met her husband, whom I'd met before anyway. I rang her up before I left because I really did want to go and talk to her and get some dialogue going about what happened all that time ago. I really felt that I needed to do it. But, unfortunately, she said that she didn't have time to see me, but that if she did she'd get in touch. But she didn't, and I have a feeling that she felt a bit uncomfortable, but I don't know. So that's an unfinished thing, really.

All that seems a long time ago now – 1985 when I first went back to New Zealand and then in 1988 for another short visit. I'm not out to my family there but I think my sister and brother know really. I did come out to my cousin in 1990 when she was here and that was OK. I get on fine with all my children, my daughter lives in London now and my two sons both have their own places in Luton and we see each other regularly.

SALLY MAXWELL

I had a conventional upbringing, a conventional adolescence. I thought that the reason why I wasn't interested in boys when all my friends seemed to be boy mad, was that I was academic, that I was going to university, and they were all just going to find husbands and settle down. I was going to be different. And I'd put that down to my academic interest, not to my sexuality. And then I went to college and liked my work, and was very busy in it. Then everybody started pairing up. And everybody seemed to be getting married, and I got married. And I can't tell you how I got married, it was just like the water going down the plughole, you're sort of just drawn towards it and there you go.

I look at these wonderful women who tell how they realised what was going on, how they had affairs in their teens and so on, and they actually did things. I think that's so dynamic, so brilliant. And I just drifted along, with the sort of social current, and it took me ages to actually name it, and say this is right for me. But eventually I did, so it's better late than never.

I was very surprised when I met Rachel and fell in love with her. I thought people didn't do that sort of thing, and that, you could say, was the time when I realised I was a lesbian. I'd left my husband – I always said I would when the children grew up – but he was a bit

147

surprised. I was living on my own, in a Quaker community in Central London, and Rachel got in touch with me from a work point of view. So, whether it was then that I was free to suit myself, and whether time had changed, I'm not quite sure; but when I look back over my life, my feeling is that I could always have known, only for a long time I had never allowed myself to know it. All my really powerful friendships had been with women.

When I met Rachel, it was just the amazing experience of falling in love, and thinking I'm forty-seven, forty-eight whatever, and I'm falling in love for the first time. And having this amazing experience, and finding it very exciting and very scarey and just suddenly thinking, this is amazing, what a surprise. And thinking also I might have gone through life and missed this completely, it might never have happened to me.

Oh, it was wonderful, absolutely wonderful. And then, of course, you think 'Well, this is absolutely idiotic: here's this elderly woman who can't walk very far, who is very eccentric and in some ways drives me completely bananas; yet you know she's wonderful. How do you reconcile these things?' And then you think 'It's like *A Midsummer Night's Dream* – I've fallen in love with Bottom and I'm going to wake up in a little while.' And then you think 'Well, it isn't – it's a relationship and I want to spend a lot of time, I want to spend all my life with this person. It's amazing. How did I come to be so lucky?' And all these thoughts are sort of washing round in your head. And other things – like 'How am I going to tell my mother and father? What are people going to think?' But you get to the point where you think, 'Well, even if it's all a dreadful mistake, I'll give it a go because it's so nice.'

I think a lot of the problem about homosexuality in our society is lack of imagination. You never see anybody in any early stages of a relationship, and all sexual activity is very private anyway, and so your mind boggles. You think 'Well, what about her boobs, anyway – they're going to get in the way!' You can't envisage it. And so when

148

it came to actually getting into bed, I got all sort of panicky. I didn't know what to do or what to expect or anything like that. And I was absolutely all of a tremble, well it was hilarious – we only had this bed which was *minute*, and I'm large and long. We just kept falling out of this bed the whole time. It was just like a comedy show and that's the way we survived, I think, just by laughing about it. We were both absolutely terrified, and anxious, and frightened and we sort of covered it up. A bit of a joke was what got us through. It was a mixture of ecstasy and embarrassment, in more or less equal quantities. I think it's lovely, I do think that Rachel's wonderful in bed – she's so cuddly – it's absolutely marvellous. It's a pleasure; every day I think, 'Mmmm, this is nice. You go through all your life, you come up to fifty and you realise you've never fallen in love before; and, what's more, so many times it could happen that you'd fall for somebody, and they'd already be attached. What amazing good luck to find the person unattached and your love being reciprocated. It's phenomenal! Absolutely.

My kids are brilliant. They have been wonderfully supportive. They were very helpful when our marriage split up, they encouraged me to leave home really. And they've taken it in their stride very well.

I got accepted to do a Quaker post in Ireland. They gave me a long time to finish things off in my other job, and during that time I met Rachel, and when I went over to Ireland, I said, 'I've now got a new relationship and I want to bring Rachel with me.' And it was awful. It was really dreadful, because they couldn't bring themselves to say, 'Look, you can't be a lesbian and do the sort of work we want you to do in Belfast.' They kept saying things like, 'Oh, she'd have to use the toilet, and she's too old.' They wouldn't come out with anything straightforward, but in the end they wrote to me and said 'We are readvertising the post, and hope you will hand in your notice.' So I had to find another job. I was very upset by it, because I think I was a bit naïve really. I was so pleased about what had happened to me, I was telling people about it. And in fact one or two people have said,

149

'Oh, well, I wouldn't mention that if I were you.' And sort of warned me off it. But I hadn't really expected this kind of rejection. I thought everyone would share my good fortune, that I had met someone that I wanted to live with, that they'd be pleased, but it didn't seem to work out like that.

Although I'm in my fifties, I haven't had this back history of things being bad. I think I accepted my lesbian position at a time when it was easier to do so and so I thought, well, blow that for a laugh, I don't want all this kind of closet business. You might as well say what you are. And in a way, the Clause 28[1] business has really strengthened my determination over that. I think you've got to then make yourself visible as an ordinary person, not as some kind of a freak.

I applied for a job with Camden and I decided right from the start I would say to them what my sexual orientation was, so that there would be no messing about, and no misunderstanding. One of the reasons why I went and worked for the London Borough of Camden was because at the bottom of their ads they have a thing about being equal opportunities employers, and they actually mentioned that they welcomed applications from gay and lesbian people – and that was such a positive thing, that I applied for work with them.

So really, working as an organiser with a family centre was the first time I'd had a job where everything was perfectly straightforward. With the families I didn't want to go out of my way to tell people about my sexuality because in an ordinary way, heterosexual people don't explain their sexual orientation. On the other hand, I never felt I had to practice any deception of any kind and people gradually realise you are a lesbian because you're talking about going on the march, or you're talking about issues. And it's just there as a fact, that you have a partner who's a woman, and so, if she comes to a party or something, everyone can see who your partner is. It's quite obvious.

I think you get some parents who've got anxieties about homosexuals. It's been very important for me to have gay men on the staff, so that parents can see that there are all kinds of people who can care for their children, and that their sexuality isn't a threat to children. Perhaps being a lesbian is slightly easier – people aren't quite as panicky about you doing something dire to their children – they just think you've got a different lifestyle. But I think you get the occasional parent who's a bit anxious about it – who doesn't quite know how to handle it. It's partly because they're fed a diet of all sorts of bizarre attitudes from the popular press. I think it's important that they get to know you first as a person, and then when they hear about your sexuality second, they can cope with it. And I don't think it's such a good idea to go round feeling that the first words you say to people are 'I'm a lesbian.' It's part of who you are, it's part of a whole pattern of other things.

An awful lot of people still say to me, 'Oh, the person you live with', 'Your flat mate' and they don't want to look at the double bed in our flat. They want to talk about two old ladies living together, because that's a pattern that's very, very common that they can cope with. They think 'Oh, yes, well, that's all right, we know about that. We know about two friends, or two retired teachers or something, buying a house together. It makes economic sense, it makes social sense. But let's not talk about any of the other personal issues.'

It was very interesting when Rachel and I did a workshop about our work with children to speech therapists in Eastbourne, and we talked about each other, they kept saying we were throwing it in their faces. Whereas I know perfectly well that if I'd said 'My husband and I did this' it would have been totally neutral, something they wouldn't have noticed. But because we were a lesbian couple, it stuck out to them, and therefore they felt that we were being aggressive about it. I think that was a very good indicator of how society feels – that they feel that you are throwing things at them, because you are actually mentioning it. What they would rather was that we just never mentioned anything at all. It's only at moments like that, when people suddenly respond in such a way, that you realise all the processes that are going on in their heads.

I'm always surprised when I go on these marches about Clause 28 and it's seen as a powerfully gay issue, because to me it's a human rights issue. It may be that the target is homosexuality, but it's really about people's liberties being taken away. It's about people's opportunities to live their lives how they want without being seen as a menace, or without being criminalised, or even marginalised.

It's excellent to be living at a time where sexuality is of interest, and you can explore all sorts of possibilities and where you can be and do all sorts of things. I don't want to be an outrageous sort of person, I don't think I am. But it's a time when things are expanding, there are possibilities. You can feel the genuine sense of freedom to explore who you are at a time when you can look back at your past, and think about your future, and see positives. And that's really good.

oo —— oo —— oo —— oo

Looking at the break up of my relationship with Rachel, I think all these things have a dramatic moment that you can find a date in the diary and say that was it. But when you look at them they've always got a much slower thing going on beforehand so there are two stories you can tell, one of which is the more dramatic event and the other which is the slow build-up to it that made it possible.

I think there is the fact that Rachel didn't want me to go with her to Moscow when she wasn't at all well. I would've been happy to go with her. The fact that she hadn't come with me when we planned to go away in the summer before; the fact that she'd cancelled her birthday party which I'd arranged for her. These were all indications, if you like, that the relationship was folding and perhaps they were the more obvious dramatic things, but all the rest of it was just falling apart. Emotionally life had become impoverished, because we had a routine, you know, coming in getting the meal, playing a card game in the evenings.

152

She wasn't sharing with me some of the things that were her preoccupations and concerns. That was important, that she wasn't open, in fact, that she wasn't honest. I know she wanted to talk, but she couldn't bring herself to. She'd often say she wasn't angry about something when it was obvious that any sensible person would be angry. Then the anger would come out in some different way and that was very difficult to handle.

There was an impasse about our perceptions of each other. I think it's terribly complicated. There are ways in which Rachel wanted me to be different from the way I was, that I didn't agree with. There were things where she wanted me to be different where I did agree. But I think I became what I'd always feared I'd be, the kind of grey person behind the scenes, the person who looks after someone, is sort of hovering about, has no life of their own, they're just a kind of shadow.

I think for her, she's always said work comes first, that's the most important thing. Everything was subservient to that, she made no bones about it, she's never kidded me, she never said I love you, she'd always said the work's the most important thing and I think she reckoned that was fair enough. I don't think she ever fell in love with me in the way I fell in love with her and that was how it was.

When I first knew I had fallen in love with somebody else, I told her. I can remember she was in bed. I came back. I hadn't meant to tell her, I'd meant to wait until I was sure about my feelings but, in a way, I did that for a few days and it just didn't seem respectful to her. I'd done that with my husband for years and years, and it seemed very easy. I thought well I can do this, I can handle it, I can lead a double life, I've kept affairs going, there's no problem, but somehow, with Rachel, I didn't want to do that and so I told her. I said, 'I've fallen in love with someone,' and she said, 'I know.' That's typical Rachel, she would say that. I don't know whether she knew or not. And then I just cried; it was awful.

I think she said when it happened, 'Oh, I never thought you'd have the guts to leave me.' So in a way I think she started respecting me much more then and that was very odd and very painful to experience – that someone admires you for actually in the end saying 'this won't do any more, I'm not having it'. And the tragedy is that we couldn't say that and sort it out before it ever got to that point.

We've had one or two get-togethers since. I've been much more assertive with her. It's such a shame I couldn't do that before, but at the end I sort of kissed her goodbye and said, 'I've learnt a lot, I admire you as a person. I'm just not living with you any more and I'm living with somebody else.'

Rachel is an amazing person, I mean she is used to transitory relationships and, although I wasn't, I didn't feel guilty about her in a way because I thought she will come up smiling, she'll come up with something, she'll make this into a positive experience, and, in fact, she has. She's been positive about it, she's learnt from it which I think is also amazing in someone who is in her eighties.

I think people are all hooked up on this idea that the only good relationship is a permanent relationship. I don't want to rubbish my relationship with Rachel at all. It was a learning experience and it had all sorts of powerful moments. It's ended and we are not living together. That's felt very liberating and has liberated acres of time and acres of my personality and probably hers as well. I think we wring our hands and say 'Oh the relationship's failed,' as if because it comes to an end it somehow wasn't any good. I'd say to people 'Life is full of wonderful encounters, some of them last longer than others, some are short and some are long and they can have good things and bad things. This was a terrific relationship, that I enjoyed, and got a lot out of, and which infuriated me, and which caused me pain, and which was very difficult, and which eventually fell apart.' So what am I saying about it? It's 'Have experiences, live a bit, don't be frightened that something might not work out.' When I wrote my first declaration of love to Rachel, I said, 'Maybe this is like *A Midsummer Night's Dream* and you're Bottom and I'll wake up, you know.' I don't think that's what happened. I think slowly cracks widened and difficulties came and we didn't face up to them, because we didn't want to. Eventually I catapulted into a decision, but I think if I'd thought what a silly thing to do, I'll never do this, I would have missed so much. What actually happened was that I had that relationship, we had over five years living together, that was a MIRACLE on its own, and I wouldn't have missed it for the world. OK, it's ended now, but I think relationships are organic, they're not fixed, and it would have been awful if I'd dragged out years of resentment and stuck it out thinking, 'I can't leave her now, I've got to wait until she dies,' for heaven's sake. I wouldn't do that to Rachel. I wouldn't stay with her and not feel this is a really positive experience. I think she deserves something better than that and I think the quality of our relationship was such that we were able to end it. And to me, having been stuck in a ghastly marriage for twenty-four years, that is a big compliment to her. I would say, 'Have it, however bizarre, HAVE the relationship, LIVE it and when it's over, it's over, and you don't have to wring your hands about that.' I really think that, I really do.

NOTES

1. *See Note 2 after the introduction.*

MARIE

I didn't call myself a lesbian until about ten years ago, but I've had relationships with women for years and years. When I was twenty-one I had an affair with a woman and that was back in the West Indies, but we didn't have a word for what went on between us. We were good friends and sometimes shared the same bed, and it just happened without our really talking about it. We just reached out and touched. It was one of those things that happened. It felt OK to me, and it was the first really grown up experience I'd had. It just went on happening, and lasted for about a year, until I came to England. I left Barbados nearly thirty years ago, and the word 'lesbian' wasn't used there then. They were called 'Wicca'. It wasn't until I had been in England for several years that I heard the word 'lesbian'.

I came here to work because there was a lot of unemployment in Barbados and I couldn't find a job that paid a decent wage. At that time, I kept the house and did the cooking at home and worked as a dressmaker, but I was getting fed up with that and with not earning very much. I went to the employment agency to sign on and they said, 'Where do you want to work, here or abroad?' and I said, 'Anywhere.' At that time there was a big recruitment for England. A few weeks went by and I was interviewed to come to England to work

157

for London Transport in 1960. I was nearly twenty-two years old.

I worked in a bus garage and was busy learning the job and settling in, but it was lonely. I had no family here, but a lot of boys from home came over to work in the garages, so I used to meet people I knew that way. Life was very tough for me, but I don't regret coming here, not really. It's all experience. I was here twelve years before I could afford to go home.

I've always been attracted to women, but it was very difficult to make contact, and I didn't hear about lesbians until many years after I arrived here. When I first came to England I didn't know where to go and meet people anyway. Also, there was a lot of racial prejudice for me to cope with, and I didn't get to meet many white women. But it was also difficult to meet other Black women, because most of them were married or in relationships with men. I think that at that time it was very difficult for white women to be out as lesbians, but for Black women it was difficult even to be single and independent. I was lonely and eventually I started relationships with men.

I had my next relationship with a woman in 1968, and again it just sort of 'happened'. She was married and after a while went back to her husband. I had two children by this time, and I was bringing them up on my own which was a real struggle, believe me, but they are grown up now, and I'm proud of them.

Then I had a relationship with a man on and off for ten years. But I did realise I had this attraction for women and I used to think 'What's wrong with you, girl?' I didn't tell anyone, it was all happening inside of me. I was struggling with my sexuality for three or four years, before I did anything about it. I'd been trying to work it out but didn't know where to go, what to do, how to meet other women. I was in my thirties then, and I just struggled on. More and more I began to think that I'm sure I fancy women and was beginning not to want this man around with whom I was having a relationship. I was working with this woman and we became really friendly. She was having problems with her husband, and she used to talk to me

158

about it, and come and cry on my shoulder. We'd talk about everything, really – sex, lesbians, gays, everything, you know. It was the sort of friendship where you could talk about anything, and gradually I realised that I was falling in love with her. I thought, 'Oh, God, what do I do about this?' I was teaching her the book side of the job, and she'd come into my office every afternoon, and our chairs would be close together and our legs would touch, and I'd get to the point where I'd have to walk out. It got really bad and I'd come home and try to work it out and think this is really desperate. But she was the type I could talk to about it, even though I knew nothing would come of it. I could tell her about it somehow and I worked out what to say. The next day, I said, 'Something really awful's happened.' And she started guessing all these things and she said, 'Are you in love with someone?' And I said 'Yes, but it can't be, it's impossible.' And she started going through all my friends that she'd heard me mention saying things like 'Is it your friend's husband?' and, because we'd talked about lesbians and sexuality and all that, I said, 'It's a woman.' 'Oh well,' she said, 'if that's the way you feel.' And she accepted it. So she said, 'Well, who is it? Can't you tell her or stop seeing her or something?' And I said, 'It won't work out, it's impossible because she doesn't feel the same way,' and stuff like that. And she said, 'Well, stop seeing her.' So I said 'OK, then, get out of my bloody office.' And she gave me a great big hug and a kiss and we just talked about it. But she understood. I just had to get it out of my system and it was really good after that, because she knew we could be OK about it. And we're still friends now.

My daughters were very good at sport and belonged to an athletics club. I became a very active committee member. I met a woman there, who was also involved in athletics, and we got to know each other quite well. She was someone I could talk to about the conflicts I was having about my sexuality. And then I saw these programmes on television about gays and lesbians, and somebody had sent in a letter in which she said that she liked men but kept having these feelings for

159

women. I cut it out and kept it because I thought, 'That's me, that's just how I feel.' When my friend came round, I showed it to her. We talked about it and also about my feelings for my friend at work and she hugged me and said, 'You poor thing, what you must have been going through!' And we became really good friends. She said, 'There's nothing wrong with it – do something about it.' So I bought *Gay News* and looked at the clubs and started going there. At first, I was a bit nervous, because I walked into *Sappho*[1] on my own and also this club, The Aztec, on my own. It was hard and I wouldn't do it now, but I was just desperate to meet other lesbians. After a while it was OK, and I met lots of people and made friends.

Before I was a lesbian, I wasn't sure what feminism was, but as a one-parent family I've always been strong and supported women's rights. As a lesbian, I became more politically aware and going to the Older Lesbian Network[2] (OLN) has helped. I just wish I could meet more older Black lesbians. I met three or four at the Black Lesbian Conference, but I suppose they have their lives sorted out and don't need organisations like the OLN which is all white, but I do; so I go.

At discos and other events that I go to, there are lots of young Black lesbians, but very young. I met a lot at the conference and we chat when I see them around, but I don't socialise much with them because of the age difference. I am proud to be an older Black lesbian, but I don't know many others. I am sure that there must be many in London, and I just wish I knew how we could contact each other.

I'd like to come out to all my friends and relatives, but I know there'd be problems. When the stuff about Martina (Navratilova) being a lesbian came out and my sister-in-law was talking about it, I said, 'Well, that's the way she is.' And my sister-in-law said, 'But it's wrong in God's eye. The Bible thing and all that. It's not natural, you know.' And I thought, 'Oh, God, here we go.' I felt that I would never be able to come out to my family. Coming out at work is difficult, because you're the same person you were yesterday, but to them you're somebody different. I don't really know what their

160

reaction would be if they found out that I am a lesbian. I haven't really discussed it with them, but on the other hand, I haven't actually hidden it from them. I mean, I talk quite openly about my friendships with women and about my social life.

NOTES

1. *See Note 4 after Jackie Forster's story.*
2. *Older Lesbian Network, c/o Wesley House, 4 Wild Court, London WC2B 5AU.*

Rachel Pinney was born in 1909 into a typical landed gentry family in Dorset. On her mother's side were distinguished scientists, including Lister, and on her father's side, generations of Empire builders.

She was educated at a private, progressive co-educational school and then at St. Felix, a public school for girls. She went to the universities of Bristol, Sheffield and King's College, London and did not obtain a degree since nobody realised she was dyslexic. She finally passed her medical exams at the ninth attempt and qualified as a General Practitioner. In 1949 she set up her practice in Chelsea for eleven years.

In 1960 she started the idea of 'Creative Listening': a method of reconciliation for people of opposing views, which she toured Europe and America to promote. This method was then adapted for children and became known as 'Children's Hours'. She has done work and written a book on the breakthrough of an autistic child and was sent to prison in 1969 for helping a fourteen-year-old boy leave the country. The law claimed she had 'kidnapped' him because she did not get his mother's permission, although Rachel had been fostering him (not legally) and was responding to his needs.

Now, aged eighty-two, Rachel lives in London and continues to teach her method of creative listening.

Eleanor was born in London in 1915 and educated at state schools. She received a scholarship to spend a year at agricultural college. After graduation, she worked on the land for ten years before joining the Civil Service, retiring as an executive officer.

Ceri Ager was born in 1916 into a middle-class family where she had a happy childhood. Up to the outbreak of war, she did not have to work and so did voluntary tasks such as V.A.D. nursing and reading to the blind. After the war she travelled a lot, finally settling down to work in London. In the sixties, she was involved with the

Minorities Research Group and producing *Arena 3* magazine. Now wheelchair-bound, she does voluntary work at the London Lighthouse and sits on a number of committees.

Ellen was born in 1920. Aged twelve, she joined a dancing troupe called the Beams Breezy Babes. She attended various schools whilst touring, before leaving at fourteen to dance in the chorus lines of West End musicals. She became the 'Head Girl' for impresario Jack Hylton until the outbreak of war, when she toured with ENSA and small companies headed by Arthur Askey. On the death of her father, during the Blitz, she was released from ENSA to care for her mother and sister. Phyllis Dixey then engaged her at the Whitehall Theatre. She worked with the Tillers Touring Troupe until she travelled to South Africa with the Ivor Novello Show. She married there but left her husband almost immediately to return to England where she gave birth to a daughter in 1950. She worked as a film extra and ran a dancing school in Clapham. To gain supplementary income she worked in various jobs, including at Marks and Spencer, the BBC Wardrobe Department, and as an occupational therapy aide at Westminster Hospital. Following serious heart disease in 1979, she retired.

Vick Robson was born into a working-class family in Kent in 1920 and grew up in a mining village in the North East where her mother came from. She went to a local school until the age of fourteen and took a job in service at Stanmore for five years. She joined the WAAF in 1940 and remained there for the duration of the war. She then held a variety of jobs in factories, as a postwoman and as a barmaid. She married against her will and left her husband to bring up her children on her own. She now lives in Newcastle, near her daughter and family, and has a good relationship with them all, including her son and three grandchildren.

Pat James was born in London in 1921 into an Anglo-Italian family. She was a market worker from the age of eight. Acting as 'little mother' to her two siblings, she was released from these responsibilities when the younger children were evacuated in 1939. She volunteered for the LAAS and worked as a driver for three years. She then joined the WAAF and has spent her life almost exclusively in the company of women. She started to write poetry at the age of sixty-two and is hoping to be 'discovered'.

Sylvia 'I was the first child of parents in their early thirties. My brother was born when I was four and a half and we had a happy childhood, though somewhat sheltered. We both won scholarships to the local grammar school and subsequently went to university. I graduated in 1943, obtaining a BA degree with second class honours in English. The following year I took a diploma in education.

'During my second year at university, I began to attend a High Anglican church and was confirmed. The vicar was homoerotic but celibate, and there was a strong bond between us. At that time I had never been out with a boy, but I had some female friends of various ages. I also had a close relationship with my brother.

I knew that I should not marry and thought I might become a nun. Accordingly, I found a teaching appointment in a convent school, but did not stay long as I became disillusioned with the Mother Superior and sisters.

'After that I had various teaching posts in boarding and day schools. Although I liked teaching, my life seemed unsatisfactory and I became depressed, so I had two years psychotherapy, during which my analyst tried to make me heterosexual, without success.

'When I was twenty-nine, I decided to try my vocation in an Anglican convent. I was a postulant there for three months, but did not feel able to be clothed as a novice as I had become emotionally involved with the Novice Mistress and feared the consequences. So I left the convent and went back to teaching. Eventually, I became head

165

of the English department in a girls' grammar school. When the school went comprehensive and co-educational, I moved to a girls' boarding-school then to another girls' day school, where I taught until I retired.'

Pat G. was born in 1922. She left school at fourteen and worked in a variety of jobs including working in an ice cream factory and a boys' prep school, until she joined the ATS in 1939. She was invalided out in 1943 and became a clerk in the Civil Service. She then held a range of secretarial positions before becoming a nurse in 1950. She entered a convent for six years and, on leaving, worked as a nurse, midwife and health visitor until she took early retirement in 1975. She now does a great deal of voluntary work.

Sharley McLean was born in Germany in 1923 and educated there, in Switzerland, and in Italy. She came to England in 1939 as a refugee. She trained and worked as a nursery nurse and later became an SRN at Lewisham Hospital. She married and had two children and, to fit with her childcare responsibilities, held an assortment of jobs from being a dresser to a ballerina, to night nursing. She worked in a safe and boring job in the school health service and did other courses to relieve the monotony, including one on family planning and orthodontics. After retirement in 1983, she became involved in voluntary work and is now a volunteer counsellor for the Terence Higgins Trust.

Ruth Magnani was born in Southampton in 1925 to an Anglo-French family. Her father was a politician and she had a conventional upbringing and education. From 1943–45 she worked with ENSA and married in 1947. She has three children, the eldest of whom is autistic. In 1968 she began a career in journalism and advertising and later worked in residential care in the Social Services. She had her first lesbian experience in 1969 and met her present partner in 1972.

Jackie Forster was born in London during 1926 to Scottish parents. She spent the first six years of her life in India, where she acquired a brother.

Jackie went to Wycombe Abbey School until it was commandeered by the American Airforce. Jackie evacuated to St Leonards School, St Andrews. Until 1945 she experienced terror of the air raid sirens, anxiety for her mother driving ambulances in the London blitz while grieving over the disappearance of her husband, a Jap POW, who turned up suddenly in September 1945. Escapism for Jackie was to play lacrosse and hockey for Scotland against England and to join the Wilson Barrett Repertory Company playing Edinburgh, Glasgow and Aberdeen until 1950 when she came to London. She was in various indifferent West End productions and half-a-dozen films. She became involved in television in the early days at Alexandra Palace graduating to her own spot and programmes as a visual reporter of news events in the UK and Europe. When ITV started she presented and featured in many programmes. At this time she stood as prospective Liberal Parliamentary candidate for Cheltenham, was married and divorced. From 1956–1964 she toured the States and Canada every autumn and appeared on all the North American TV networks. She lived in Toronto from 1962–64 then returned to Britain to work for Border Television until 1968. As a political activist, she co-founded and edited *Sappho* magazine for ten years and gave up a nerve-wracking career as a performer under her own name – Jacqueline Mackenzie. Involved in the women's and gay movements she represented lesbians in London as a member of the Women's Committee of the GLC in the 1980s.

Currently she is working as office manager for the British School at Rome in London and is Vice-Coordinator of the local tenants association.

Diana Chapman was born in Bristol in 1928. She was educated at Colston Girls' School, Bristol and then took a course in social studies at Bristol University. She moved to Australia and studied at Sydney University to become a dentist. She retired in 1988 after thirty years in NHS dentistry.

Betty was born in 1929. Her father was a chartered accountant and her mother was a teacher. She was educated at Channing School, Highgate; Herts and Essex High School; St. Teresa's Convent, Effingham; and Guildford Polytechnic. She graduated from the Royal College of Veterinary Surgeons in London in 1952 and practised in Brighton from 1952 to 1954. She has two daughters and is a grandmother. Since her marriage she worked part-time in various jobs – as a librarian, for the Citizen's Advice Bureau, training kennelmaids, running a dog grooming service, ambulance driving for people with disabilities, painting dog portraits in oils, as a hospital Dental Surgery Assistant for which she qualified in 1986, and gardening.

She took up golf at forty-three, canoeing at fifty-five, hiking at sixty; and is a keen birdwatcher. She has lived and travelled in the USA; coffee-harvested in Nicaragua in 1987; trekked in Nepal in 1990, and visited Australia in 1991.

She supports initiatives for peace, human rights and the environment.

Rosanna Hibbert was born in 1932 and educated by governesses and at schools in the Sudan, Kenya and England. She trained as a singer at the Guildhall School of Music and Drama. She became a copywriter in 1957 and in 1970 started to learn a new trade as a television director, remaining at the BBC for seventeen years. She is now a freelance writer.

Nina Miller 'An only child, I was born in Jersey in 1933 and lived there until I was almost seven when we evacuated because of the war, ending up in Yorkshire. After a time, my father joined the RAF and I lived with my mother in Wakefield and Halifax. We returned to Jersey a year after the war and I left the island again at eighteen to train as a teacher in Bath and London.

'I taught first in South London then in Kenya for three years. I travelled back to England overland down the Nile from Uganda to Egypt then to Athens, Crete, Italy and back to Crete where I lived for six months.

'On my return to England, I taught in Essex and London. At the end of my teaching career I had the headship of a junior school for six years. During this last job, I trained as a counsellor.

I gave myself early retirement at the age of fifty for two major reasons so that I could take up my creative interests again (art, craft and writing), and also to be out as a lesbian – I was tired of being closeted in my professional life.

'I saved enough to live simply, without working for a couple of years and planned to work part-time after that. When my father died I was able to pay for further therapy training.

'I chose to live in Brighton as it has good art facilities, a large lesbian population and I already had contacts with counsellors there. I am currently working part-time as a counsellor and studying for a Certificate in Art (Embroidery).'

Dorothy Dickson-Barrow was born in the Caribbean in 1934. She came to Britain for one year and, so far, has stayed for thirty-four years! She has been a midwife, a health visitor, teacher, health promotion officer and is now a training officer. She has been trying for years to increase the visibility of Black people and to put them on the agenda in both the education and health services. She is, and will continue to be, a Black activist for women, Black people and for Black lesbians in particular.

Jan Russell 'I was born in Wellington, New Zealand, in 1935, one of ten children, eight of whom survive. My mother was born in England and was a war bride of the First World War.

I left school at the age of fifteen, worked for two years in an office and then became a student nurse for two years. I left New Zealand in 1956 for England and in 1960 I was married in London. In 1966 I moved to Luton and lived there for sixteen years, having three children, one daughter and two sons. In 1978 I became involved in the Women's Movement and belonged to an action group.

In 1980 I came out as a lesbian, later leaving my marriage and going to Hillcroft College in Surbiton. After leaving Hillcroft I lived and worked in London. In 1985 I returned to New Zealand for five months, the first time I had been there since leaving in 1956. I then returned to London where I began working with Pensioners Link and became involved with development work with the older lesbians. I am now fifty-six, and thinking of future retirement, and am looking forward to moving to Norfolk in the near future, with my partner Sally. I am looking forward to changing my life again and following up my interests in older lesbians, birdwatching, walking, and having a good 'bop' occasionally.

Sally Maxwell was born in 1936. She attended a girls' PNEU school and transferred to a girls' grammar school for the sixth form. After a degree course at Royal Holloway College, London, she entered the teaching profession. She married and went to teach in West Africa with her husband, where her two children were born. They returned to England in 1966 where Sally completed an M.Ed and started a playgroup which recreated the sociable African style of child-rearing which she missed in England. She developed an interest in Early Years which absorbed her for the rest of her professional life. She tutored playgroup courses, worked as a borough administrator in Hackney, as an advisory teacher of the Early Years for Dorset LEA and became national advisor to the Pre-School Playgroups Association in 1979.

170

On leaving the PPA, she managed a Children's Centre in Camden and then joined ILEA as head of the Child Care Unit. She has now taken early retirement and is working as an assistant officer of a Devon County Council Children's Home. In 1966, she joined the Society of Friends and has done various jobs in the organisation. She has been actively involved in the Peace Movement, especially at Greenham and at Molesworth, as a result of which she has served two short custodial sentences.

Marie is a Black lesbian mother and grandmother. She was born in Barbados in 1939 but has lived most of her life in England. She is independent, has a demanding job and enjoys a happy and committed relationship with her lover, Ruth. Her main interests are in Black and feminist issues and she is keen to meet other older Black lesbians to share experiences and to socialise.

Following the 19... communism and socialism, Croire in... but is now disillusioned to ... of the child ... C.T.M. Weeks now lives ... caught up ... and is working at an art school where she has ... Groupe of... Christ ... At time, to ... the importance of ... friends and literature ... Also to the recognition ... she has not only ... with the Free Age Movement ... actually ... Christian and ... Violet ... as a result of which ... has become involved as a social ... service.

Violet is a ... both a mother and grandmother. She was born in ... in 19-4 but has lived most of her life in England. She is a qualified ... has done ... and is obviously happy and content in ... stimulating with her peers ... and. She is often in demand to speak to... and to ... conferences and to societies.